Vegetal Visitor 2009

Edited by Annemarie Weitzel

Jon Carpenter

to Shetlands

This edition first published 2009 by
Jon Carpenter Publishing, Alder House, Market Street, Charlbury, Oxfordshire OX7 3PH
Tel and fax: 01608 811969 E-mail: vv@joncarpenter.co.uk
This compilation © Annemarie Weitzel
Whilst the publishers must disclaim responsibility for any inaccuracy, the information in
this guide has been carefully checked at the time of going to press
ISBN 978-1-906067-04-5
Printed and bound by CPI Antony Rowe, Chippenham

Contents

How to use this guide   6

Activity Holidays, Special Breaks, Courses   9

1   London and Middlesex   13

2   South and South East   19
    Dorset (East), Hampshire, Isle of Wight, Kent, Surrey, Sussex

3   West Country   28
    Cornwall, Devon, Dorset (West), Somerset and Bristol,
    Wiltshire

4   Thames and Chilterns   43
    Bedfordshire, Berkshire, Buckinghamshire, Hertfordshire,
    Oxfordshire

5   East Anglia   45
    Cambridgeshire, Essex, Norfolk, Suffolk

6   East Midlands   48
    Derbyshire, Leicestershire, Lincolnshire, Nottinghamshire

7   Heart of England   51
    Gloucestershire, Herefordshire, Shropshire, Warwickshire,
    West Midlands, Worcestershire

8   North East England   58
    Cleveland, Durham, Northumberland, Tyne & Wear, Yorkshire

9   North West England   66
    Cheshire, Cumbria, Isle of Man, Lancashire incl. Greater
    Manchester and Merseyside

10 Wales   78
    North Wales, Powys, South Wales, West Wales

11 Scotland   89
    Aberdeenshire & Moray, Argyll, Ayrshire, Borders, Dumfries &
    Galloway, Edinburgh, Glasgow and Central Scotland, the
    Scottish Highlands, Shetland Islands, the Western Scottish Islands

Further vegetarian information   105

VisitBritain offices abroad   111

How to use this guide

Welcome to the new edition of *Vegetarian Visitor*, listing private houses, guest houses, hotels, cafés, restaurants and pubs which take catering for vegetarians and vegans seriously. All establishments in the guide have been supplied with a 'We're in Vegetarian Visitor 2009' sticker, to make them easily recognisable.

Activity holidays, Special breaks, Courses

Entries are listed alphabetically by county, then name. Almost all offer bed and breakfast: 'see also page XX' tells you where to find further details, including websites and email addresses.

Accommodation and Eateries

Entries are grouped geographically in sections and within each section alphabetically by county, then town or village, then name. London is divided into Central, East, North, South and West and entries are arranged first by postcode (i.e. NW3, W1, WC2, SW16), then alphabetically by name.

Accommodation addresses have coded information as well as a general description. The codes indicate the following:

H	Hotel	**G**	Guest House	**PH**	Private house

INS   Inspected under one of the schemes operating in Britain; full details can be obtained from the establishment concerned if required

L   Licensed

DA   Disabled access

V   Exclusively vegetarian: entries without this code also cater for non-vegetarians

Ve   Also catering for vegans; please mention you are a vegan when you contact the establishment

Vegan   Exclusively vegan

NS   No smoking anywhere on the premises (may include garden)

pNS   Smoking restricted to certain areas only

CN   Car necessary: a car/taxi journey or extended walk is needed from the nearest public transport

Acc2   Accommodation for two adults; children travelling with their parents can sometimes be accommodated additionally

Price categories for bed and breakfast per person per night (minimum, guide only):

CatA over £37.50; **CatB** £25-£37.50; **CatC** under £25.

Many cafés, restaurants and pubs have a short description, as well as coded information. Opening times may vary not only by establishment but also by season. As a general rule, cafés will be open during the day but not in the evening, and are often closed on Sundays and Bank Holidays. Restaurants are generally open for lunch and in the evening; they may be closed one day a week, but this is not usually Sunday. Pubs are normally open seven days a week and may be open all day and in the evening. If you want to be sure that your chosen eating place is open, please give them a ring. The codes give the following information:

R	Restaurant	**C**	Café	**P**	Pub
L	Licensed				

a   A selection of vegetarian dishes daily, as well as non-vegetarian food; quite often at least one vegan dish is also on the menu
b   Vegetarian food only
c   Vegetarian and vegan food only
d   Vegan food only
w   Wholefood
org   Organic produce used when possible

As England, Wales and Scotland have a ban on smoking in public places, which includes restaurants, cafés and pubs, all premises are smoke-free.

I would be delighted to hear from any user of this guide. If you have stayed or eaten somewhere not listed, please drop me a line with the name and address and I will contact them for next year's edition.

Annemarie Weitzel
2 Home Farm Cottages, Sandy Lane, St Paul's Cray, Kent BR5 3HZ
e-mail: a.weitzel@live.co.uk

Activity Holidays, Special Breaks, Courses

England

Nab Cottage
☎ 015394 35311, fax 015394 35493

Rydal, Ambleside, Cumbria LA22 9SD

Retreat breaks, workshops and courses in yoga, dance, massage, transforming cellular memory. The workshop/venue space in the attached barn is ideal for groups, yoga, dance, walking, celebrations. See also page 69.

Rothay Manor
☎ 015394 33605, fax 015394 33607

Rothay Bridge, Ambleside, Cumbria LA22 0EH

We offer the following types of specialised holidays: antiques, bridge, chess, gardening, Lakeland life – past and present, music, painting, scrabble, walking. See also page 66.

Devon Valley Retreat
☎ 01548 821180

Lower Norris House, North Huish, South Brent, nr Totnes, Devon TQ10 9NJ

Feeling stressed?? Unwind in beautiful, hidden Devon valley. Aromatherapy massage, reflexology and spiritual healing available. Healing, painting and other courses held occasionally. Groups welcome. See also page 34.

Tor Cottage
☎ 01822 860248, fax 01822 860126

Chillaton, Devon PL16 0JE

We are a Romantic Retreat and a special place for Birthdays, Anniversaries and Honeymoons. Special Autumn-Spring Breaks available, offering one night free of charge, or 10% discount on a 7-

night holiday throughout the year. No children. No smoking. No pets. See also page 32.

Polemonium Plantery ☎ 01429 881529

28 Sunnyside, Trimdon Grange, Trimdon Station, Durham TS29 6HF

We offer Vegetarian Cookery, Green Family Activity and Cycling/Walking weekends. See also page 58.

Cheltenham Lawn ☎ 01242 526638

5 Pittville Lawn, Cheltenham, Gloucestershire GL52 2BE

We run art design, drawing, textile and mixed media printmaking courses. See also page 51.

Claridge House, Quaker Centre for Healing, Rest and Renewal

☎ 01342 832150, fax 01342 832140

Dormans Road, Dormansland, Lingfield, Surrey RH7 6QH

Open all year for stress releasing peaceful stays, retreats and courses with a healing focus. See also page 22.

Bishops Wood Environmental Education Centre ☎ 01299 250513

Crossway Green. Stourport-on-Severn, Worcestershire DY13 9SE

This unique centre is one of the best examples of environmental design and construction techniques in the country and attracts visitors from far and wide. It provides courses ranging from willow sculpture to environmental management for industry and from woodland survival crafts to reed-bed treatment of sewage! For further information please contact the Head of Centre at the above address. Accommodation can be found at Tytchney Gables, just 1½ miles away, and Mrs Margaret Peters can also provide information about activities at the Centre and about the Friends of Bishops Wood group. See page 57.

Wales

Bronwen Cottage
☎ 01248 450533

Rhoscefnhir, Pentraeth, Anglesey LL75 8YS

Join us for our yoga, plant-based raw & living foods and how to make biodiesel courses. See also page 79.

Heartspring
☎ 01267 241999

Hill House, Llansteffan, nr Carmarthen, Carmarthenshire SA33 5JG

We run healing and therapeutic residential retreats by the sea, with a choice of complementary therapies and delicious organic vegetarian food. We also have vegetarian self-catering apartments for peaceful holidays. See also page 86.

Over the Rainbow
☎ 01239 811155

Plas Tyllwyd, Tanygroes, nr Cardigan, Ceredigion SA43 2JD

We offer nature/walking weekends, courses in bellydancing, salsa and Reiki and scrapbooking/craft workshops. Over the Rainbow is licensed for Civil Ceremonies. See also page 87.

Awen Vegetarian B&B
☎ 01495 244615

Penrhiwgwair Cottage, Twyn Road, Abercarn, Newport, Gwent NP11 5AS

Please ask about our courses in Reiki I, II and III. See also page 84.

Cuffern Manor
☎ 01437 710071

Roch, Haverfordwest, Pembrokeshire SA62 6HB

Contact us for walking, cycling, art, craft, birdwatching, fungus spotting and music holidays. See also page 87.

Elan Valley Hotel
☎ 01597 810448, fax 01597 810824

Elan Valley, Rhayader, Powys LD6 5HN

We organise wild mushroom foraging, bird watching, watercolour landscapes and life drawing special breaks with expert tutors. See also page 82.

Primrose Earth Retreats ☎ 01497 847636

Primrose Farm, Felindre, Brecon, Powys LD3 0ST

Quiet retreats are offered for de-stressing. Sound healing (UK College of Sound Healing) courses are also available. See also page 82.

Scotland

White Rock Bed & Breakfast ☎ 01546 870310

Leac Na Ban, Tayvallich, nr Lochgilphead, Argyll PA31 8PF

Please ask about our arts and crafts courses, taught by local and visiting artists. If required group bookings of up to 8 can be accommodated (sharing rooms). See also page 91.

Creag Meagaidh B&B ☎ 01540 673798

Main Street, Newtonmore, Inverness-shire PH20 1DP

If you are interested in a running, walking, wildlife, skiing, cycling or multi activity holiday please contact us. See also page 100.

Fournet House Accommodation

☎ 01340 821428

Balvenie Street, Dufftown, Moray AB55 4AB

These will be a new venture for 2009. Please contact Alison for exact details. She is hoping to teach and hand on her knowledge in Nutrition and cooking particularly relating to cancer, Interior design and soft furnishing, The practical application of colour, and Gardening as a therapy. Other experts will expand the programme. Dip into interesting books, enjoy interesting talks and enjoy the whole Fournet experience. See also page 90.

Woodland ☎ 01549 441715

Rosehall, by Lairg, Sutherland IV27 4BD

We offer yoga holidays. See also page 101.

London

Central London

Lincoln House Hotel

☎ 020 7486 7630, fax 020 7486 0166

33 Gloucester Place, London W1U 8HY

e-mail: reservations@lincoln-house-hotel.co.uk
website: www.lincoln-house-hotel.co.uk

See display ad below.
H INS CatB Ve pNS Acc50

Cafés, restaurants, pubs

Carnevale Restaurant ☎ 020 7250 3452
  135 Whitecross Street, London EC1Y 8JL   R L c org

GABY'S

30 Charing Cross Road

London WC2H 0DB

Tel: 020 7836 4233

Tas Restaurant ☎ 020 7430 9721/9722
37 Farringdon Road, London EC1M 3JB   R L a org
Zen Garden ☎ 020 7242 6128
88 Leather Lane, London EC1N 7TT   R/C L c
The Place Below ☎ 020 7329 0789
St. Mary-le-Bow Church, Cheapside, London EC2V 6AU   C c
Beatroot ☎ 020 7437 8591
92 Berwick Street, Soho, London W1V 3PP
A budget healthy vegetarian feast at Beatroot. Tofu stir-fry, Jamaican
curry, home-baked quiche, seasonal salads. Any selection of hot food
and salads, £3.90 small, £4.90 medium, £5.90 large. Fresh superfood
smoothies, delicious cakes. www.beatroot.org.uk   C c
Govinda's Pure Vegetarian Restaurant ☎ 020 7437 4928
9 Soho Street, London W1D 3DL   R c
La Porte des Indes ☎ 020 7486 6002
32 Bryanston Street, Marble Arch, London W1H 7EG   R L a
Mildreds ☎ 020 7439 2392
45 Lexington Street, Soho, London W1F 9AN   R L c

Gaby's Deli ☎ 020 7836 4233
30 Charing Cross Road, London WC2H 0DE
See display ad on page 14.   R L a w
World Food Café ☎ 020 7379 0298
1st Floor, 14 Neal's Yard, Covent Garden, London WC2H 9DP   C c

East London

Cafés, restaurants, pubs

Rootmaster ☎ 07912 389314
Ely's Yard, The Old Truman Brewery, Hanbury Street, London E1 6QL
                                                             R L d org

Wild Cherry ☎ 020 8980 6678
241-245 Globe Road, London E2 0JD
See display ad below.   R c
Pogo Café ☎ 020 8533 1214
76A Clarence Road, Hackney, London E5 8HB
Fully vegan, mostly organic, volunteer-run co-operative. Wednesday-
Sunday 12.30-9pm. www.pogocafe.co.uk   C d org

North London

Cafés, restaurants, pubs

Jai Krishna Vegetarian Restaurant ☎ 020 7272 1680
161 Stroud Green Road, Finsbury Park, London N4 3PZ
A well established, family-run vegetarian restaurant (BYO) and take-away, providing a variety of delicious dishes from all over India.   R c

Rasa N16 ☎ 020 7249 0344
55 Stoke Newington Church Street, London N16 0AR   R L b

Café Seventy Nine ☎ 020 7586 8012
79 Regents Park Road, London NW1 8UY   C b w org

Green Note ☎ 020 7485 9899
106 Parkway, London NW1 7AN   R L c

Madder Rose Café
Triyoga, Unit 4, 6 Erskine Road, Primrose Hill, London NW3 3AJ
C c org

Manna Restaurant ☎ 020 7722 8028
4 Erskine Road, Primrose Hill, London NW3 3AJ   R L c org

South London

Bed and Breakfast Putney

☎ 020 8785 7609, fax 020 8789 5584

1 Fanthorpe Street, Putney, London SW15 1DZ

e-mail: bbputney@btinternet.com
website: www.bbputney.com

Pip and Robert Taylor give a unique British experience in London. Our rooms are comfortable and reasonably priced. There is easy access to the centre. Putney has one of the best riverside locations, with restful and attractive walks.
PH CatA Ve NS Acc4

Cafés, restaurants, pubs

Tas Pide ☎ 020 7928 3300
20-22 New Globe Walk, London SE1 9DR   R L a

Tas Restaurant ☎ 020 7403 7200
72 Borough High Street, London SE1 1XF   R L a

Mulberry Tea Rooms ☎ 020 8856 3951
Charlton House, Charlton Road, Charlton, London SE7 8RE   C a
Domali Café ☎ 020 8768 0096
38 Westow Street, Crystal Palace, London SE19 3AH   C L a
Shahee Bhelpoori ☎ 020 8679 6275
1547 London Road, Norbury, London SW16 4AD   R L c

West London

Temple Lodge   ☎ 020 8748 8388, tel/fax 020 8748 8322
51 Queen Caroline Street, Hammersmith, London W6 9QL

e-mail: templelodgeclub@btconnect.com
The tranquility of this large house, former home of the artist Sir Frank Brangwyn, is described as a peaceful haven by visitors. It dates back at least to Georgian times. A view over the large secluded garden is enjoyed from both library and dining room, where the hearty buffet breakfast is served. Most bedrooms, all with washbasins, desks and tea-making, look onto the garden and have a Scandinavian touch: two have showers en-suite, a shower room and 3 bathrooms serve the others. The West End and the City are accessible by tube and bus, as is the more leafy open country in Richmond and Kew.

G INS CatA V Ve NS Acc18

Cafés, restaurants, pubs

The Gate Vegetarian Restaurant ☎ 020 8748 6932
51 Queen Caroline Street, Hammersmith, London W6 9QL   R L c org
222 Veggie Vegan Restaurant ☎ 020 7381 2322
222 North End Road, London W14 9NU   R L d w org
Hollyhock Café ☎ 020 8948 6555
Terrace Gardens, Richmond Riverside, Richmond TW10 6UX
Beautiful little café with verandah overlooking Thames in Victorian flower garden. Salads, pastries, soups, ices and chilled drinks served all day.   C c

Tide Tables ☎ 020 8948 8285
Riverside, Richmond TW9 1TH
Wonderful setting on banks of River Thames at Richmond. Delicious
salads, bakes and snacks, smoothies, ice cream and gourmet coffees
and teas served all day.   R/C c org

Middlesex

Cafés, restaurants, pubs

Good Veg ☎ 020 8357 1740
62 High Street, Edgware HA8 7EJ   R c
Mr Man Vegetarian Chinese Restaurant ☎ 020 8905 3033
236 Station Road, Edgware HA8 7AU
See display ad below.   R c
Pradip's Vegetarian Restaurant ☎ 020 8909 2232
156 Kenton Road, Harrow HA3 8AZ   R c
Pallavi South Indian Restaurant ☎ 020 8892 2345
Unit 3, Cross Deep Court, Heath Road, Twickenham TW1 4QJ   R L a

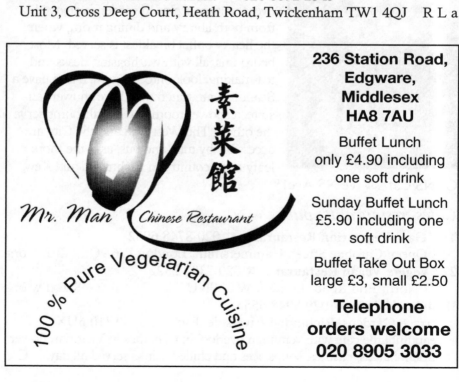

South and South East

Dorset (East)

Cowden House
☎ 01300 341377

Frys Lane, Godmanstone, Dorchester DT2 7AG

website: www.cowdenhouse.co.uk

A spacious house on the edge of a little village, with beautiful views and surrounded by rolling downland. We provide a peaceful environment with comfort, personal attention and the highest quality vegetarian food, using local organic produce wherever possible.
PH CatB V Ve NS Acc6

Cafés, restaurants, pubs

The Salad Centre ☎ 01202 393673
  667 Christchurch Road, Bournemouth BH7 6AA   C c w org
Wessex Tales Vegetarian Restaurant ☎ 01202 309869
  20 Ashley Road, Boscombe, Bournemouth BH1 4LH   R L d
Filippo's Italian Restaurant ☎ 01202 738031
  222 Ashley Road, Parkstone, Poole BH14 9BY   R L a

Hampshire

The Barn Vegan Guest House
☎ 023 8029 2531

112 Lyndhurst Road, Ashurst SO40 7AU

e-mail: info@veggiebarn.net
website: www.veggiebarn.net

We offer exclusively vegan accommodation in a unique and beautiful

area of the UK. We provide holidays with a light environmental footprint by, for example, generating nearly all of our electricity and using chemical-free household products.
G CatB Vegan NS Acc4

Cafés, restaurants, pubs

The White Horse ☎ 01489 892532
Beeches Hill, Bishops Waltham SO32 1FD P L a
Red Mango Café ☎ 023 9248 0113
Havant Arts Centre, East Street, Havant PO9 1BS C/Bar L a

Isle of Wight

Brambles ☎ 01983 862507

10 Clarence Road, Shanklin PO37 7BH

e-mail: vegan.brambles@virgin.net
website: www.bramblesvegan.co.uk

See display ad on page 21.
G CatB Vegan NS Acc14

Cafés, restaurants, pubs

The Cameron Tea Rooms ☎ 01983 756814
Dimbola Lodge, Terrace Lane, Freshwater Bay PO40 9QE
Situated within Dimbola Photographic Galleries and Museum, offering a selection of both vegetarian and non-vegetarian food.
www.dimbola.co.uk C a
Quay Arts ☎ 01983 822490
Sea Street, Newport PO30 5DB C L a org

Cafés, restaurants, pubs

Café Mauresque ☎ 01227 464300
8 Butchery Lane, Canterbury CT1 2JR   R L a
The Good Food Café ☎ 01227 456654
Above Canterbury Wholefoods, 1-2 Jewry Lane, Canterbury CT1 2RP
Open Tuesday-Saturday 9-5, Sundays 12-4. Breakfast, lunch, drinks,
snacks and takeaways. Daily changing menu, using the finest local,
organic vegetables available.   R/C c w org
The India Restaurant ☎ 01303 259155
1 The Old High Street, Folkestone CT20 1RJ
Authentic traditional Indian home cooking. Freshly cooked, grease-
free and prepared to order.   R L a
What The DickInns Public House ☎ 01634 409912
1 Ross Street, Rochester ME1 2DF
See display ad on page 23.   P L a org
Brockhill Country Park Café ☎ 07798 752555
Sandling Road, Saltwood, nr Hythe CT21 4HL
Junction 11 off M20. Children's play area, a beautiful lake, walks and
savoury food at savery prices. We are open 10.30-5.30 April to October,
10.30-4 November to March, closed 22 December-4 January.   C c

Surrey

Claridge House ☎ 01342 832150, fax 01342 832140
Dormans Road, Dormansland, Lingfield RH7 6QH
e-mail: welcome@claridgehouse.quaker.eu.org
website: www.claridgehouse.quaker.eu.org

Victorian country house, beautiful
gardens. Open all year for peaceful
stays, retreats, courses with a healing
focus. Vegetarian food. Vegan and
certain medical diets available with
notice. Disabled access, ground floor
bedrooms, no single person
surcharge, 46 minutes London

Victoria. See also page 10.
G CatA DA V Ve NS CN Acc17

WHAT THE DickInns

Feel confident the food served here really *is* vegetarian. Brenda, joint proprietor and strict vegetarian, prepares the food herself and also provides a limited menu for your carnivore friends! Wheelchair friendly and only 4 minutes from Rochester High Street with an attractive garden for eating al fresco with a glass of organic wine on those balmy evenings.

For further information contact Brenda or Graham on ~ 01634 409912 ~ "What the DickInns Bar", Ross Street, Off Delce Road, Rochester, Kent ME₁ 2DF

Cafés, restaurants, pubs

Riverside Vegetaria ☎ 020 8546 7992/0609
64 High Street, Kingston upon Thames KT1 1HN   R L c org

For restaurants in Richmond, Surrey, please see under West London on page 17/18.

Sussex

Dacres
☎ 01323 870447

Alfriston, East Sussex BN26 5TP

Pretty country cottage in beautiful gardens in picturesque village. Sleeps two/three. Organic vegetarian breakfasts. En-suite bathroom. Colour TV. Tea/coffee making facilities. Near to South Downs Way, Glyndebourne, Seven Sisters, Charleston Farmhouse, village pubs, restaurants. Wonderful walking country. PH INS CatB Ve NS CN Acc3

Paskins Hotel
☎ 01273 601203, fax 01273 621973

18/19 Charlotte Street, Brighton, East Sussex BN2 1AG

e-mail: welcome@paskins.co.uk
website: www.paskins.co.uk

See display ad on page 24.
G INS CatA Ve NS Acc34

The Royal Hotel
☎ 01323 649222

8-9 Marine Parade, Eastbourne, East Sussex BN21 3DX

e-mail: info@royaleastbourne.org.uk
website: www.royaleastbourne.org.uk

See display ad on page 26.
G INS CatA V Ve NS Acc20

Jeake's House

☎ 01797 222828

Mermaid Street, Rye, East Sussex TN31 7ET

e-mail: jeakeshouse@btinternet.com
website: www.jeakeshouse.com

See display ad on page 27.
G INS CatA L Ve NS Acc22

Cafés, restaurants, pubs

Food for Friends ☎ 01273 202310
  17-18 Prince Albert Street, The Lanes, Brighton, East Sussex BN1 1HF
                                                              R L c w org
Infinity Foods Café ☎ 01273 670743
  50 Gardner Street, Brighton, East Sussex BN1 1UN   C c w org
Iydea Vegetarian Kitchen ☎ 01273 667992
  17 Kensington Gardens, Brighton, East Sussex BN1 4AL   C L c

Jeake's House

Beautiful listed building dating from 1689, in mediaeval cobblestoned street. Traditional or vegetarian breakfast served in 18th-century galleried former chapel.

Oak-beamed and panelled bedrooms, with brass, mahogany or four-poster beds. En-suite bathrooms, hot drinks trays, televisions. Four-poster honeymoon suite and family room available.

Own private car park, £3.00 per day.

VisitBritain 5 Star Gold Award
Les Routiers Bed and Breakfast of the Year
Oldie Magazine Best Breakfast Award
Good Hotel Guide César Award

Tel 01797 222828
Fax 01797 222623
jeakeshouse@btinternet.com

Mermaid Street, Rye, East Sussex TN31 7ET

www.jeakeshouse.com

Terre à Terre Restaurant ☎ 01273 729051
  71 East Street, Brighton, East Sussex BN1 1HQ
  Award winning restaurant with knock-your-socks-off food, organic
  wine list and great service. Website www.terreaterre.co.uk   R L c org
Café Paradiso ☎ 01243 532967
  5 The Boardwalk, Northgate, Chichester, West Sussex PO19 1AR

C c

St Martin's Organic Tearooms ☎ 01243 786715
  3 St Martin's Street, Chichester, West Sussex PO19 1NP   C L a w org
Wealden Wholefoods Co-op ☎ 01892 783065
  High Street, Wadhurst, East Sussex TN5 6AA   C L c w org

West Country

Cornwall

Coast
☎ 01736 795918

St Ives Road, Carbis Bay, St Ives TR26 2RT

e-mail: info@coastcornwall.co.uk
website: www.coastcornwall.co.uk

Stylish B&B, exclusively vegetarian and vegan, all rooms en-suite, stunning sea views and garden. Home to the hugely popular Bean Inn Restaurant and Wild Planet Art Gallery. Close to St Ives beaches, restaurants and galleries.
G CatB V Ve NS Acc16

Westaways
☎ 01822 833745

Latchley, nr Gunnislake PL18 9AX

e-mail: westaway.westaway@googlemail.com

2½ miles from Gunnislake, 6 miles from Tavistock and 20 miles from Plymouth and Bude, a lovely two double bedroom 17th century cottage. B&B, lunches and evening meals optional. Walks and meditation on a quiet peaceful retreat.
PH CatB V Ve pNS CN Acc4

The Yellow House
☎ 01872 553168

41 Vicarage Road, St Agnes TR5 0TG

e-mail: yellowhouse41@gmail.com
website: www.stagnesyellowhouse.co.uk

Small friendly vegetarian/vegan B&B in the heart of the village. 'Excellent! Spotless rooms and a warm welcome. Veggie breakfast

cooked with love!' St Ives, Penzance and the Eden Project are less than an hour away. Evening meals available.
G CatB V Ve NS Acc4

The Great Escape ☎ 01736 794617
16 Parc Avenue, St Ives TR26 2DN

website: www.g-escape.freeuk.com

Chintz-free B&B fifteen minutes from the Tate Gallery. Stunning views of St Ives Harbour and Bay. En-suite rooms with TV and CD players. Full breakfasts including freshly squeezed orange juice, full veggie/vegan fry-up and home-made yoghurt and muesli.
G INS CatB V Ve NS Acc8

Making Waves ☎ 01736 793895
3 Richmond Place, St Ives TR26 1JN

e-mail: simon@making-waves.co.uk
website: www.making-waves.co.uk

Making Waves have scaled back on the B&B accommodation they offer for 2009 whilst bringing up their young family, but do now offer self-catering accommodation in two beautiful apartments with gardens, with the same stunning views and 2-
minute walk to the harbour. B&B off-season by arrangement. No more evening meals, but St Ives is spoilt for veggie-friendly cafés and restaurants Simon can point you towards!
Self-catering/G off-season INS CatB Vegan NS Acc6

Michael House
☎ 01840 770592

Trelake Lane, Treknow, Tintagel PL34 0EW

e-mail: info@michael-house.co.uk
website: www.michael-house.co.uk

Vegetarian and vegan guest house, near Tintagel, beach and coastpath nearby, lovely scenery and views, great sunsets. Evening meals, relaxing atmosphere, friendly and welcoming, open all year. Special Christmas breaks and spring and autumn offers. Children and pets welcome.
G CatB L V Ve NS Acc6

Boswednack Manor
☎ 01736 794183

Zennor, St Ives TR26 3DD

e-mail: boswednack@ravenfield.co.uk
website: www.boswednackmanor.co.uk

Peaceful farmhouse and self-catering cottage in far West Cornwall. Lovely views from all rooms. Library, organic gardens, friendly hens, sea sunsets. Wonderful walks from the door, secret coves, birds, wildflowers, stone circles. Pub ½ mile. Sorry, no dogs.
G INS CatB V Ve NS Acc10

Cafés, restaurants, pubs

The Bean Inn ☎ 01736 795918
Coast B&B, St Ives Road, Carbis Bay, St Ives TR26 2RT
See display advert on page 31.   R/C c org

Pea Souk Café ☎ 01326 317583
19c Well Lane, Church Street, Falmouth TR11 3EG
Falmouth's only vegetarian café is owned and run by a Cordon Vert graduate. Pea Souk specialises in Middle Eastern mezze. See display advert on page 31.   C L c w org

The Golden Lion Inn and Lakeside Restaurant ☎ 01209 860332
Stithians Lake, Menherion, nr Redruth TR16 6NW   R/P L a

Archie Browns Café ☎ 01736 362828
Old Brewery Yard, Bread Street, Penzance TR18 2EQ   C L c w org

Waves Restaurant ☎ 01841 520096
Higher Harlyn, St Merryn, Padstow PL28 8SG   R/C L a

The Crooked Inn ☎ 01752 848177
Stoketon Cross, Trematon, nr Saltash PL12 4RZ — P L a org
Fodders Restaurant ☎ 01872 271384
Pannier Market, Back Quay, Truro TR1 2LL — R L a w
Lettuce and Lovage ☎ 01872 272546
15 Kenwyn Street, Truro TR1 3BU — R/C L c org

Devon

Cuddyford B & 'BEES'   ☎ 01364 653325
Rew Road, Broadpark, Ashburton TQ13 7EN

e-mail: a.vevers@csl.gov.uk
website: www.ashburton.org/directory/cuddyford

Rural setting within Dartmoor
National Park. Ideal for exploring
Dartmoor, Dart Valley and South
Devon coastline. Wholesome
cookery – home-baked bread, free-
range eggs, honey from our own
hives, organic fruit and vegetables.
Special diets catered for. Children
are welcome.
PH INS CatB V Ve NS CN
Acc4+children

Tor Cottage   ☎ 01822 860248, fax 01822 860126
Chillaton PL16 0JE (Tavistock/Dartmoor area)

e-mail: info@torcottage.co.uk
website: www.torcottage.co.uk

Nestling in private valley,
relaxed romantic atmosphere.
Luxurious beautiful bedsitting
en-suites with own log fires
and private gardens in
streamside setting. Superb
vegetarian breakfasts. Vegetarian owner. RAC 5 Diamonds Little Gem

Award, National winner ETC Gold Excellence Award, 2002 All England Winner of AA Best Accommodation Award. Heated outdoor pool. Brochure available. Early booking advisable. See also page 9.
H INS CatA Ve NS CN Acc10

Fern Tor Vegetarian and Vegan Guest House
☎ 01769 550339

Meshaw, South Molton EX36 4NA

e-mail: veg@ferntor.co.uk
website: www.ferntor.co.uk

Surrounded by splendid countryside. Relax in our 12 acres or explore Exmoor, North and Mid-Devon. En-suite. Cordon Vert host. Pets welcome. Voted Best Vegan Accommodation 2007, and one of *The Guardian*'s 10 Best UK Vegetarian B&Bs 2008.
G CatB V Ve NS Acc6

Sparrowhawk Backpackers
☎ 01647 440318

45 Ford Street, Moretonhampstead, Dartmoor National Park TQ13 8LN

e-mail: ali@sparrowhawkbackpackers.co.uk
website: www.sparrowhawkbackpackers.co.uk

Beautifully converted stone stable, this is a small friendly, charming, eco-hostel located in the village of Moretonhampstead. A convenient base to explore the atmospheric Dartmoor National Park. Hiking, cycling, mountain biking, climbing, and wild swims here for the adventurous traveller. There is a fully equipped kitchen, solar heated showers, bike shed and lovely courtyard. Individuals, groups, families. Dorm or double room.
PH INS CatC DA Acc18

Devon Valley Retreat ☎ 01548 821180

Lower Norris House, North Huish, South Brent, nr Totnes TQ10 9NJ

e-mail: touchofheaven888@yahoo.co.uk
website: www.devon-valley-retreat.co.uk

Unwind in tranquil, green valley 8 miles from Totnes. Enjoy the lovely views from the house or relax by the log fires. Wonderful walking area. Delicious vegetarian/vegan home cooking, special diets catered for. Healing, massage and other therapies available on request. See also page 9.

PH INS CatB V Ve NS CN Acc6

Berkeley's of St James ☎ and fax 01752 221654

4 St James Place East, The Hoe, Plymouth PL1 3AS

e-mail: enquiry@onthehoe.co.uk
website: www.onthehoe.co.uk

Quiet exclusive bed & breakfast offering free range/organic food where

possible. Ideally situated on the Hoe, walking distance to Sea Front, Historic Barbican, Ferry Port, Theatre, Pavilions and City Centre and within travelling distance of the Eden Project and Dartmoor National Park.

G INS CatA DA NS CN Acc10

The Old Forge at Totnes   ☎ 01803 862174
Seymour Place, Totnes TQ9 5AY

e-mail: enq@oldforgetotnes.com
website: www.oldforgetotnes.com

A warm and friendly 600-
year-old stone building with
cobbled drive and coach arch
leading into a walled garden.
Quiet and peaceful, yet close
to town centre and river.
Newly refurbished, cottage-
style rooms, conservatory
lounge with whirlpool spa. Parking.
Laptop users: free broadband internet access via wireless hot spot.
G INS CatA L Ve NS Acc24

Overcombe House   ☎ 01822 853501, fax 01822 853602
Old Station Road, Horrabridge, Yelverton PL20 7RA

e-mail: enquiries@overcombehotel.co.uk
website: www.overcombehotel.co.uk

Comfortable, friendly, non-smoking 4 Star guest house with 8 en-suite
bedrooms. Views over the Walkham Valley towards the High Moors.
Easy access to Tavistock, Buckland Abbey and The Garden House.
Serving local and homemade produce. B&B from £32.50 pppn.
G INS CatB L DA NS Acc15

Cafés, restaurants, pubs

The Terrace Café ☎ 01626 832223
   Devon Guild of Craftsmen, Riverside Mill, Bovey Tracey TQ13 9AF
                                                      C L a w org
The Courtyard Café & Wholefood Shop ☎ 01647 432571
   76 The Square, Chagford TQ13 8AE   C c w org
Herbies Restaurant ☎ 01392 258473
   15 North Street, Exeter EX4 3QS   R L c w org

The Plant Café-Deli ☎ 01392 428144
1 Cathedral Yard, Exeter EX1 1HJ
Contemporary vegetarian and organic food. Private dinner parties and outside catering available. Finalists in 2005 Vegetarian Society Awards 'Best Café'. C c w org

The Country Table Café ☎ 01626 202120
12 Bank Street, Newton Abbot TQ12 2JW R/C a w

Peter Tavy Inn ☎ 01822 810348
Peter Tavy, nr Tavistock PL19 9NN
See display ad above. P L a

The Green Room ☎ 01752 202616
Plymouth Arts Centre, 38 Looe Street, Plymouth PL4 0EB
R/C L a w org

Willow Vegetarian Garden Restaurant ☎ 01803 862605
87 High Street, Totnes TQ9 5PB R L c w org

Dorset (West)

Cafés, restaurants, pubs

The Green Yard Café ☎ 01308 459466
4-6 Barrack Street, Bridport DT6 3LY   R/C L a
Broadwindsor Craft and Design Centre ☎ 01308 868362
Broadwindsor, nr Beaminster DT8 3PX   R L a w
Pilot Boat Inn ☎ 01297 443157
Bridge Street, Lyme Regis DT7 3QA   P L a

Somerset and Bristol

Lavender House   ☎ 01225 314500
17 Bloomfield Park, Bath BA2 2BY

e-mail: post@lavenderhouse-bath.com
website: www.lavenderhouse-bath.com

See display ad below.
G INS CatA Ve NS CN Acc9

Marlborough House ☎ 01225 318175, fax 01225 466127
1 Marlborough Lane, Bath BA1 2NQ

e-mail: mars@manque.dircon.co.uk
website: www.marlborough-house.net

See display ad above.
G INS CatA L DA V Ve NS Acc16

Number 30 ☎ and fax 01225 337393
30 Crescent Gardens, Bath BA1 2NB

e-mail: david.greenwood12@btinternet.com
website: www.numberthirty.com

Three minutes' level walk to historical city centre and private parking. Victorian, non-smoking house with a clean, contemporary feel. Comfortable, light en-suite bedrooms. Superb English or great vegetarian breakfasts. 'Outstanding housekeeping with a warm welcome.' Weekends 2 night minimum.
G INS CatA Ve NS Acc8

Tordown B&B and Healing Centre

☎ 01458 832287, fax 01458 831100

5 Ashwell Lane, Glastonbury BA6 8BG

e-mail: torangel@aol.com
website: www.tordown.com

Victorian house situated on the southern slopes of Glastonbury Tor. Warm welcoming sacred space, in which you can relax and enjoy your stay. Beautiful rooms with tea, coffee, herbal tea, TV, en-suite. Healing and hydrotherapy spa available. Sumptuous vegetarian/vegan breakfast provided. VB 4 Stars. G INS CatB V Ve NS CN Acc14

Parsonage Farm

☎ 01278 733237

Over Stowey, Bridgwater TA5 1HA

e-mail: suki@parsonfarm.co.uk
website: www.parsonfarm.co.uk

Traditional 17th-century farmhouse and organic smallholding in the Quantock Hills. Friendly and informal, with delicious meals using farm's produce, home-made breads and jams. Peaceful village, log fires and walled gardens make your stay a relaxing break, while being ideally situated for rambling and exploring the unspoiled Quantock Hills, Exmoor, North Somerset coast, Glastonbury and Wells. G INS CatB Ve NS CN Acc6

Cafés, restaurants, pubs

Demuths Vegetarian Restaurant ☎ 01225 446059
  2 North Parade Passage, off Abbey Green, Bath BA1 1NX
  Bath's only vegetarian restaurant, lots of vegan choices, organic wines. Good Food Guide recommended. Open for breakfast, lunch, tea and dinner. www.demuths.co.uk   R L c

The Porter ☎ 01225 404445
  15 George Street, Bath BA1 2EN
  See display ad below.   P L c
Sally Lunn's Refreshment House ☎ 01225 461634
  4 North Parade Passage, Bath BA1 1NX   R L a
Tilleys Bistro ☎ 01225 484200
  3 North Parade Passage, Bath BA1 1NX
  Family-run city centre bistro close to Bath Abbey. French and English
  cooking. Yummy vegetarian dishes. Gluten-free options available.
  www.tilleysbistro.co.uk   R L a
Walrus & Carpenter ☎ 01225 314864
  28 Barton Street, Bath BA1 1HH   R L a
Yum Yum Thai Restaurant ☎ 01225 445253
  17 Kingsmead Square, Bath BA1 2AE   R L a org
Café Kino ☎ 0117 924 9200
  3 Ninetree Hill, Bristol BS1 3SB   C L d w org

Café Maitreya ☎ 0117 951 0100
89 St Mark's Road, Easton, Bristol BS5 6HY
The UK's top vegetarian restaurant – Which Good Food Guide,
Observer Food Magazine, and the Vegetarian Society. Evenings only.
Website www.cafemaitreya.co.uk   R L c org
Friary Café ☎ 0117 973 3664
9 Cotham Hill, Cotham, Bristol BS6 6LD   C a
Krishna's Inn ☎ 0117 927 6864
4 Byron Place, Bristol BS8 1JT   R L a
Royce Rolls Café ☎ 07967 211870
The Corn Exchange, St Nicholas Market, Bristol BS1 1JQ   C c w org
Teohs ☎ 0117 907 1191
26-34 Lower Ashley Road, St Agnes, Bristol BS2 9NP   R L a
The Thali Café ☎ 0117 942 6687
12 York Road, Montpelier, Bristol BS5 6QE
Serving delicious authentic Asian speciality dishes in the heart of
Bristol for over a decade. Vegans well catered for.   R L c
Walrus & Carpenter ☎ 0117 974 3793
1 Regents Street, Clifton, Bristol BS8 4HW   R L a
Yum Yum Thai Restaurant ☎ 0117 929 0987
50 Park Street, Bristol BS1 5JN   R L a org
The Garden Café ☎ 01373 454178
16 Stony Street, Frome BA11 1BU   R/C L c w
Café Galatea ☎ 01458 834284
5A High Street, Glastonbury BA6 9DP
Established 15 years – internationally known
restaurant/gallery/cybercafé. High class vegetarian/vegan cuisine,
organic wines and beers. Open daytime and evenings.Website
www.cafegalatea.co.uk   R/C L c w org
Rainbows End Café ☎ 01458 833896
17A High Street, Glastonbury BA6 9DP   C c w org
Lotus Flower Thai Restaurant ☎ 01823 324411
89-91 Station Road, Taunton TA1 1PB   R L a w org
The Crown at Wells & Anton's Bistrot ☎ 01749 673457
Market Place, Wells BA5 2RP
Fifteenth-century inn providing affordable accommodation in central
Wells. Fabulous food served all day, with good selection of vegetarian
dishes.   R/P L a

Wiltshire

Bradford Old Windmill

☎ 01225 866842, fax 01225 866648

4 Masons Lane, Bradford on Avon, nr Bath BA15 1QN

e-mail: vegvis@bradfordoldwindmill.co.uk
website: www.bradfordoldwindmill.co.uk

A touch of romance near Bath in an ex-windmill. Dramatic position above an old Cotswold stone town, with spectacular views. Vegetarian/vegan breakfast menu 95% organic. Vegetarian dinner from around the world (Monday, Wednesday, Thursday, Saturday) 70% organic. Vegetarian proprietor. AA 5 Stars, Distinctly Different 4Ds.
G INS CatA Ve NS Acc10

Cafés, restaurants, pubs

Circle Restaurant ☎ 01672 539514
  High Street, Avebury SN8 1RF   C L c
The Bridge Tea Rooms ☎ 01225 865537
  24A Bridge Street, Bradford on Avon, nr Bath BA15 1BY   R L a w
The Bistro & Cookery School ☎ 01380 720043
  7 Little Brittox, Devizes SN10 1AR   R L a w org
The Cross Keys Inn ☎ 01672 870678
  16 High Street, Great Bedwyn, Marlborough SN8 3NU   P L a
Anokaa Contemporary Indian Cuisine ☎ 01722 414142
  60 Fisherton Street, Salisbury SP2 7RB
  An explosive fusion of exotic spices; a rich amalgam of evocative aromas; a tantalising contrast of textures and tastes. Innovative vegetarian selections cooked by a team of professional chefs. A dining experience of proper Indian vegetarians! www.anokaa.com   R L a org

Thames and Chilterns

Bedfordshire

Cafés, restaurants, pubs

Donatello's ☎ 01525 404666
  91 Dunstable Street, Ampthill MK45 2NG   R L a
Donatello's ☎ 01582 475797
  204 High Street North, Dunstable LU6 1AU   R L a
Wok n Buffet ☎ 01582 661485
  1 Tring Road, Dunstable LU6 2PX   R L a

Berkshire

Cafés, restaurants, pubs

The Swan Inn ☎ 01488 668326
  Lower Green, Inkpen, nr Hungerford RG17 9DX   R/P L a w org
Tutu's Ethiopian Table ☎ 0118 958 3555
  35-39 London Street, Reading RG1 4PS   R L a org
Misugo Japanese Restaurant ☎ 01753 833899
  83 St Leonards Road, Windsor SL4 3BZ   R L a w

Buckinghamshire

Cafés, restaurants, pubs

Carlos's Portuguese Restaurant ☎ 01296 421228
  7-11 Temple Street, Aylesbury HP20 2RN   R L a
Veggie World ☎ 01908 632288
  150-154 Queensway, Bletchley, Milton Keynes MK2 2RS   R c

Hertfordshire

Cafés, restaurants, pubs

Woody's Café ☎ 01442 266280
19 Dickinson Quay, Hemel Hempstead HP3 9WG
Beautiful location on the river. Wine and dine or just pop in for a cup
of tea.
C L c org

The Waffle House ☎ 01727 853502
Kingsbury Watermill, St Michaels Street, St Albans AL3 4SJ
R a w org

Oxfordshire

Cafés, restaurants, pubs

Café Quay ☎ 01295 270444
Banbury Museum, Spiceball Park Road, Banbury OX16 2PQ   C L a

Café @ Modern Art Oxford ☎ 01865 722733
30 Pembroke Street, Oxford OX1 1BP   C L b

Chiang Mai Kitchen ☎ 01865 202233
Kemp Hall Passage, 130A High Street, Oxford OX1 4DH   R L a

Edamame Japanese Home Cooking and Sushi ☎ 01865 246916
15 Holywell Street, Oxford OX1 3SA   R L a

Hi-Lo Jamaican Eating House ☎ 01865 725984
68-70 Cowley Road, Oxford OX4 1JB
Delicious home-cooked meals and snacks. Vegan organic dishes and
various veggie starters and side orders. Open 25 years. R/C/P L a org

The Nosebag Restaurant ☎ 01865 721033
6-8 St Michael's Street, Oxford OX1 2DU   R L a

Vaults & Garden ☎ 01865 279112
University Church of St Mary, High Street, Oxford OX1 4AH   C a org

East Anglia

Cambridgeshire

Stockyard Farm B&B

☎ 01354 610433, fax 01354 610422

Wisbech Road, Welney, Wisbech PE14 9RQ

Former farmhouse, rurally situated between Ely and Wisbech. Private
lounge. 1 twin, 1 double, both
with H&C, tea making, radios,
hairdryers. Central heating,
private parking. Pets
welcome. Ideal for
birdwatchers and general
touring, close to Welney
Wetland Centre and Ely.
PH CatB Ve NS CN Acc4

Cafés, restaurants, pubs

The Cambridge Blue ☎ 01223 471680
85/87 Gwydir Street, Cambridge CB1 2LG
Changing selection of vegetarian dishes. Enjoy with a pint of real ale
from the best selection in the area.   P L a

Charlie Chan Restaurant ☎ 01223 359336
14 Regent Street, Cambridge CB2 1DB   R L a

Rainbow Vegetarian Café ☎ 01223 321551
9A Kings Parade, opposite Kings College gates, Cambridge CB2 1SJ
World-famous, award-winning purely vegetarian and vegan restaurant,
serving international innovative cuisine in the heart of historic
Cambridge.   R/C L c

The Pear Tree Inn ☎ 01223 891680
High Street, Hildersham CB21 6BU
Changing range, minimum 3 interesting vegetarian options, plus
home-cooked vegetable pie, every evening (except Tuesday). Unspoilt
pub, idyllic village.   P L a w org

Essex

Cafés, restaurants, pubs
The Lemon Tree ☎ 01206 767337
48 St Johns Street, Colchester CO2 7AD

R L a

Norfolk

Greenbanks Hotel & Country Restaurant

☎ 01362 687742

Swaffham Road, Wendling, nr Dereham NR19 2AB

e-mail: jenny@greenbankshotel.co.uk
website: www.greenbankshotel.co.uk

Country hotel with vegetarian menu
plus meat cuisine, all using local
produce. 10 acres of lakes and meadows,
large indoor heated swimming pool, jaccuzi
and sauna. Full disabled access with luxury wet
rooms in ground floor suites. Pets welcome. Silver Awards, Green
Globe Tourism Awards, Queens Awards for Environment.
H INS CatA L DA Ve NS CN Acc22

Cafés, restaurants, pubs
The Kings Arms ☎ 01263 740341
Westgate Street, Blakeney, Holt NR25 7NQ

P L a org

Amandines ☎ 01379 640449
Norfolk House Courtyard, St Nicholas Street, Diss IP22 4LB

R/C L c

The Greenhouse ☎ 01603 631007
42-46 Bethel Street, Norwich NR2 1NR
Norwich's environment centre. Open Tuesday-Saturday 10am-5pm,
hot food from noon. Soups, savouries, cakes, fairtrade, organic and
local. www.GreenhouseTrust.co.uk

C L c w org

Norwich Arts Centre ☎ 01603 660352
St Benedicts Street, Norwich NR2 4PG

C L a

The Waffle House Restaurant ☎ 01603 612790
39 St Giles Street, Norwich NR2 1JN R L a w org
The Mulberry ☎ 01842 820099
11 Raymond Street, Thetford IP24 2EA R L a

Suffolk

Western House ☎ 01787 280550
High Street, Cavendish CO10 8AR

In lovely village, this old coaching house is well placed for visiting villages of Lavenham, Kersey and Long Melford, and for gardeners there is Beth Chatto's by Colchester. Cavendish has three pubs which serve food in the evening.
PH CatC V Ve NS Acc7

Cafés, restaurants, pubs

Six Bells Inn and Restaurant ☎ 01359 250820
The Green, Bardwell, Bury St Edmunds IP31 1AW R/P L a
The Linden Tree ☎ 01284 754600
7 Outnorthgate, Bury St Edmunds IP33 1JQ P L a
The Red Lion ☎ 01473 657799
Greenstreet Green, Great Bricett, Ipswich IP7 7DD
Family-friendly vegetarian pub, vegan and gluten-free choices. Large garden, play area, disabled access and facilities. Well-behaved dogs welcome. P L c
The Swan Inn
Low Street, Hoxne, Eye IP21 5AS R/P L a org
Kwan Thai Restaurant ☎ 01394 388338
21a New Street, Woodbridge IP12 1DY R L a

East Midlands

Derbyshire

Sheriff Lodge
☎ 01629 760760

Dimple Road, Matlock DE4 3JX

e-mail: info@sherifflodge.co.uk
website: www.sherifflodge.co.uk

Luxurious accommodation in our
guesthouse, with seven foot long beds.
Our vegetarian breakfast offers a wide
variety from which you can choose. We
also cater for vegans and coeliac sufferers.
We are only minutes from Chatsworth
and the Peak District.
G INS CatA Ve NS Acc10

Cafés, restaurants, pubs

Columbine Restaurant ☎ 01298 78752
7 Hall Bank, Buxton SK17 6EW
R a

Scarthin Café ☎ 01629 823272
The Promenade, Scarthin, Cromford, nr Matlock DE4 3QF C c w org

Outside Café ☎ 01433 651978
Main Road, Hathersage, Hope Valley S32 1DT
C L a

Caudwell's Country Parlour ☎ 01629 733185
Rowsley, Matlock DE4 2EB
C c w org

Leicestershire

Cafés, restaurants, pubs

The Good Earth Restaurant ☎ 0116 262 6260
19 Free Lane, Leicester LE1 1JX
R L c w org

Mirch Masala ☎ 0116 261 0888
Unit 19/20 Belgrave Commercial Centre, Leicester LE4 5AU   R L c

Staunton Stables Tea and Luncheon Rooms ☎ 01332 864617
The Ferrer's Centre, Staunton Harold, nr Ashby-de-la-Zouch LE65 1RU
The original Tea Room here at Staunton Harold. Tourism Award
winner, purveyors of fine food and beverages. Lunchtime reservations
recommended.   C a

Lincolnshire

Cafés, restaurants, pubs

The Five Sailed Windmill & Tea Room ☎ 01507 462136
East Street, Alford LN13 9EQ
One of the gems of rural Lincolnshire. Healthy eating in the stylish
Tea Room. Beautiful working windmill producing stone-ground
flours. Website www.fivesailed.co.uk and e-mail
enquiries@fivesailed.co.uk   C b w org
Pimento Tearooms ☎ 01522 544880
26/27 Steep Hill, Lincoln LN2 1LU
Home-made vegetarian and vegan meals and cakes, plus a comprehensive
list of leaf teas and freshly roasted and ground coffees.   C c
Thailand No 1 ☎ 01522 537000
80-81 Bailgate, Lincoln LN1 3AR
Authentic Thai cuisine, à la carte and set menus including vegetarian.
Private parties up to 35. Best Thai Select Award by Government of
Thailand. Close to the cathedral. www.thailandno1.co.uk   R L a
The Copper Kettle ☎ 01754 767298
29 Lumley Road, Skegness PE25 3LL   R L a

Nottinghamshire

Cafés, restaurants, pubs

The Alley Café/Bar ☎ 0115 955 1013
Cannon Court, Longrow, Nottingham NG1 6JE   C/P L c w org
Encounters Restaurant ☎ 0115 947 6841
59 Mansfield Road, Nottingham NG1 3FH   R L a
The Old Angel Pub ☎ 0115 947 6735
7 Stoney Street, Nottingham NG1 1LG   P L a org

Squeek ☎ 0115 955 5560
23-25 Heathcote Street, Nottingham NG1 3AG
Relaxed and friendly, in Nottingham's city centre. Serving fresh
imaginative food with organic vegan wines, beers and minerals.
R L c org

Minster Refectory ☎ 01636 815691
Minster Centre, Church Street, Southwell NG25 0HD
A selection of vegetarian dishes always available. Pre-booked parties
catered for. Outside catering also available.				R L a w

The Five Sailed Windmill,
Alford, Lincolnshire.

Heart of England

Gloucestershire

Cheltenham Lawn and Pittville Gallery
☎ 01242 526638

5 Pittville Lawn, Cheltenham GL52 2BE

e-mail: anthea.millier@cheltenhamlawn.com
website: www.cheltenhamlawn.co.uk

Regency town house, close to Pittville Park, Pump Room, town centre, racecourse. Recently refurbished, original features, four-poster bed. Conference room, art gallery. Art/textile courses available. Member of the Vegetarian Society's Food and Drink Guild. Award-winning breakfasts. Wireless internet. See also page 10.
G INS CatB V Ve NS Acc10 (children on request)

Cafés, restaurants, pubs

Balti Spice ☎ 01453 766454
   17 Gloucester Street, Stroud GL5 1QG   R L a
Mills Café Bar & Kitchen Shop ☎ 01453 884416
   Witheys Yard, High Street, Stroud GL5 1AS   C L a w org
The Wheatsheaf ☎ 01454 412356
   Chapel Street, Thornbury, nr Bristol BS35 2BJ
   Wide selection of home-made vegetarian and vegan dishes prepared
   by the vegan co-owner of this traditional pub.   P L a

Herefordshire

Somerville House ☎ 01432 273991, fax 01432 268719
12 Bodenham Road, Hereford HR1 2TS
e-mail: enquiries@somervillehouse.net
website: www.somervillehouse.net

See display ad below.
H/G INS CatA L Ve NS Acc20

Cafés, restaurants, pubs
The Pandy Inn ☎ 01981 550273
  Dorstone, nr Hay-on-Wye HR3 6AN   P L a org
Café @ All Saints ☎ 01432 370415
  All Saints Church, High Street, Hereford HR4 9AA   C L a
'Nutters' ☎ 01432 277447
  Capuchin Yard, Church Street, Hereford HR1 2LR
  See display ad on page 53.   C L c w

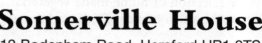

Shropshire

White House Vegetarian Bed and Breakfast
☎ 01691 658524

Maesbury Marsh, Oswestry SY10 8JA

e-mail: whitehouse@maesburymarsh.co.uk
website: www.maesburymarsh.co.uk

See display ad on page 54.
G INS CatB DA V Ve NS Acc6+2 children

Cafés, restaurants, pubs

Cinnamon Coffee & Meeting House ☎ 01746 762944
  Waterloo House, Cartway, Bridgnorth WV16 4EG   C L c w org
Acorn Wholefood Café ☎ 01694 722495
  26 Sandford Avenue, Church Stretton SY6 6BW
  Highly recommended award-winning wholefood café central in
  'walkers welcome' town. Tranquil tea garden. Open 9.30-5pm, closed
  Wednesdays.   C a w org

Berry's ☎ 01694 724452
  17 High Street, Church Stretton SY6 6BU   C L a org
Cinnamon at the Green Wood Centre ☎ 01952 432769
  Station Road, Coalbrookdale, Telford TF8 7DR   C L c w org
The Sun Inn ☎ 01584 861239
  Corfton, Craven Arms SY7 9DF
  This pub offers six vegetarian dishes and one vegan dish. Real ale on
  sale, one is always suitable for vegans and vegetarians.   P L a
The Olive Branch Restaurant & Coffee House ☎ 01584 874314
  2/4 Old Street, Ludlow SY8 1NP   R/C L a
Raphaels Restaurant ☎ 01952 461136
  4 Church Street, Shifnal TF11 9AA   R L a org
The Goodlife Wholefood Restaurant ☎ 01743 350455
  Barrack's Passage, 73 Wyle Cop, Shrewsbury SY1 1XA   R/C L c w org

Warwickshire

Monks Barn Farm   ☎ 01789 293714

Shipston Road,
Stratford-on-Avon CV37 8NA

e-mail: ritameadows@btconnect.com
website: www.monksbarnfarm.co.uk

A delightful farmhouse, offering first-
class amenities and with views across the
Stour Valley. Double, family, twin and
single rooms available, most en-suite.
Ground floor rooms in accommodation
separate to main house. Riverside walks
to the village.
G INS CatB Ve NS Acc13

Cafés, restaurants, pubs

The Vintner ☎ 01789 297259
    4-5 Sheep Street, Stratford-upon-Avon CV37 6EF   R/Wine bar L a
Saffron Restaurant ☎ 01926 402061
    Unit 1, Westgate House, Market Street, Warwick CV34 4DE   R L a
Summersault ☎ 01788 543223
    27 High Street, Rugby CV21 3BW   R/C L c w org

West Midlands

Cafés, restaurants, pubs

Jyoti Vegetarian Restaurant ☎ 0121 766 7199
    569-571 Stratford Road, Sparkhill, Birmingham B11 4LS   R c
Jyoti Restaurant ☎ 0121 778 5501
    1045 Stratford Road, Hall Green, Birmingham B28 8AS   R c
Khazana Pure Vegetarian Indian and Chinese Restaurant ☎ 0121 551 0908
    12 Holyhead Road, Handsworth, Birmingham B21 0LT   R L c

Sibila's Restaurant ☎ 0121 456 7634
Canal Square, 100 Browning Street, Birmingham B16 8EH   R L c w org
Ulysses Greek Restaurant
42A Bristol Street, Birmingham B5 7AA   R L a
The Warehouse Café ☎ 0121 633 0261
54-57 Allison Street, Digbeth, Birmingham B5 5TH
City centre oasis for vegetarians and vegans. Inexpensive good quality
food, plenty of choice in laid-back surroundings.   R/C c w org
Browns Independent Bar ☎ 024 7622 1100
Earl Street, Coventry CV1 5RU
A family owned and run bar. One minute's walk from Coventry
Cathedral. www.brownsindependentbar.com   C L a
Kakooti Italian Restaurant ☎ 024 7622 1392
16 Spon Street, Coventry CV1 3BA   R L a
Garden Organic Restaurant ☎ 024 7630 8213
Wolston Lane, Ryton on Dunsmore, Coventry CV8 3QD
See display ad below.   R L a org

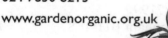

Worcestershire

Mrs Margaret Peters, Tytchney Gables
☎ 01905 620185

Boreley, Ombersley, nr Worcester WR9 0HZ

Sixteenth-century medieval Hall House cottage in peaceful country lane, 2½ miles Ombersley, 8 miles Worcester. Ideal for walking and touring. River Severn nearby and just half a mile to Ombersley Golf Course. Double, family and single

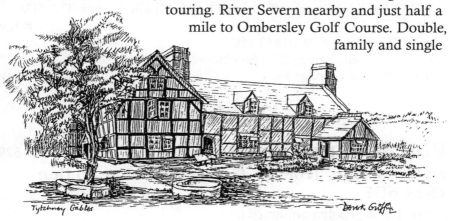

Tytchney Gables   Derek Griffin

rooms, cot available. B&B from £20. Only 1½ miles from the Bishops Wood Environmental Education Centre – see page 10.
PH CatC Ve NS CN Acc6

Cafés, restaurants, pubs

Lady Foley's Tea Room ☎ 01684 893033
  Great Malvern Station, Imperial Road, Malvern WR14 3AT   C L a
Red Lion ☎ 01684 564787
  4 St Anns Road, Great Malvern WR14 4RG   P L a org
Natural Break ☎ 01562 743275
  6 Blackwell Street, Kidderminster DY10 2DP   R/C L a
Chesters Restaurant ☎ 01905 611638
  51 New Street, Worcester WR1 2DL   R L a

North East England

Cleveland

Cafés, restaurants, pubs

Eliano's Brasserie ☎ 01642 868566
20-22 Fairbridge Street, off Grange Road, Middlesbrough TS1 5DJ

R L a

The Waiting Room ☎ 01642 780465
9 Station Road, Eaglescliffe, Stockton-on-Tees TS16 0BU
See display ad on page 59.

R L c w org

Durham

Polemonium Plantery
☎ 01429 881529

28 Sunnyside, Trimdon Grange, Trimdon Station TS29 6HF

e-mail: bandb@polemonium.co.uk
website: www.polemonium.co.uk

An environmentally-friendly (Green Tourism Gold Award) country village retreat. Family-friendly, Fairtrade, organic, with vegan toiletries. 2 miles off Cycle Route 1, 7 miles east of Durham. En-suite rooms, under 2s free with organic nappy service. See also page 10.

G INS CatB Ve NS Acc4

Northumberland

Cafés, restaurants, pubs

The Hexham Tans Restaurant ☎ 01434 656284
   13 St Marys Chare, Hexham NE46 1NQ   R L c
The Chantry Tea Rooms ☎ 01670 514414
   9A Chantry Place, Morpeth NE61 1PJ   C L a

Tyne & Wear

Cafés, restaurants, pubs

Sky Apple Café ☎ 0191 209 2571
   182 Heaton Road, Heaton, Newcastle upon Tyne NE6 5HP   R/C c

Yorkshire

Beck Hall   ☎ 01729 830332

Cove Road, Malham, nr Skipton, North Yorkshire BD23 4DJ

e-mail: alice@beckhallmalham.com
website: www.beckhallmalham.com

Eighteenth-century pet and child friendly Beck Hall welcomes visitors to the Yorkshire Dales. Situated by a stream and surrounded by countryside, there are 2 pubs nearby for dinner. Vegetarian home-cooked breakfasts and packed lunches.

G INS CatB L DA Ve NS Acc34

Costa House

☎ 01751 474291

12 Westgate, Pickering, North Yorkshire YO18 8BA

e-mail: rooms@costahouse.co.uk
website: www.costahouse.co.uk

Charming Victorian town house close to town centre. Luxurious en-
suite accommodation, equipped for your every comfort: TV, DVD
player, organic toiletries, Fairtrade teas & coffees, bathrobes, and much
more. Wireless internet connection in all rooms. Delicious vegetarian
breakfasts created for you from our extensive menu.
PH INS CatB Ve NS Acc6

Marine View Guest House

☎ 01723 361864

34 Blenheim Terrace, Scarborough, North Yorkshire YO12 7HD

e-mail: info@marineview.co.uk
website: www.marineview.co.uk

Ian and Virginia welcome you to their friendly, family-run six
bedroomed guest house. Set in a prominent position on the north cliff
overlooking the magnificent North Bay. All of Scarborough's
numerous attractions are within easy walking distance.
G INS CatC Ve NS CN Acc15

Falcon Guesthouse

☎ 01947 603507

29 Falcon Terrace, Whitby, North Yorkshire YO21 1EH

B&B in quiet location, seven
minutes' walk from centre and
harbour. Lounge and sunny
breakfast room. Organic fare. Tea
making equipment in bedrooms.
Parking near house. Whitby has
beach, historical connections, and
proximity to North York moors.
PH CatB Ve NS Acc7

Avondale Guest House ☎ 01904 633989

61 Bishopthorpe Road, York YO23 1NX

e-mail: kaleda@avondaleguesthouse.co.uk
website: www.avondaleguesthouse.co.uk

Charming 19th-century Victorian House just a few minutes' walk to York's ancient city walls. Homely en-suite rooms with extensive breakfast menu including vegetarian options. Non-smoking environment with free on-road parking. Prices from £31 pp/pn. Minimum booking two nights.
G INS CatA Ve NS Acc14

Cornmill Lodge Vegetarian Guest House ☎ and fax 01904 620566

120 Haxby Road, York YO31 8JP

e-mail: cornmillyork@aol.com
website: www.cornmillyork.co.uk

A spacious Edwardian guest house within 15 minutes' walk of York Minster. Wide choice of breakfasts using organic and Fairtrade food where possible. Vegetarian owner. Completely non-smoking. All bedrooms en-suite. Off-road carpark. Discounts for members of Viva!, Vegetarian or Vegan Society, Peta, etc.
G CatB V Ve NS Acc7

Cafés, restaurants, pubs

Prashad, Vegetarian Deli & Restaurant ☎ 01274 575893
86 Horton Grange Road, Bradford, West Yorkshire BD7 2DW
Multi-award-winning, regional and national accolades, featured in 2007, 2008 and 2009 Which Good Food Guide. See
www.prashad.co.uk   R/C c

South Square Vegetarian Café ☎ 01274 834928
South Square, Thornton Road, Thornton, Bradford, West Yorkshire
BD13 3LD   C c

The Malt Shovel Inn ☎ 01423 862929
Brearton, Harrogate, North Yorkshire HG3 3BX   R/P L a

Bean There ☎ 01262 679800
10 Wellington Road, Bridlington, East Yorkshire YO15 2BG   C c org

Brook's Restaurant ☎ 01484 715284
6 Bradford Road, Brighouse, West Yorkshire HD6 1RW   R L a
Eating Whole ☎ 01302 738730
25 Copley Road, Doncaster, South Yorkshire DN1 2PE
Small, friendly vegetarian and vegan café/restaurant with varied and
imaginative selection, all prepared and cooked on the premises.
                                                        R/C L c w org
Thai Elephant Restaurant ☎ 01423 530099
Unit 3-4, 13-15 Cheltenham Parade, Harrogate, North Yorkshire HG1
1DD   R L a
Laughing Gravy ☎ 01422 844425
The Birchcliffe Centre, Birchcliffe Road, Hebden Bridge, West
Yorkshire HX7 8DG
Licensed vegetarian restaurant, open evenings Thursdays, Fridays,
Saturdays and Sundays. Bookings only, on 01422 844425.
www.laughinggravy.co.uk   R L c
Relish ☎ 01422 843587
Old Oxford House, Albert Street, Hebden Bridge, West Yorkshire
HX7 8AH   R c
Helmsley Walled Garden Café ☎ 01439 771194
Cleveland Way, Helmsley, North Yorkshire YO62 5AH
Delicious, unusual salads, home-made soups, home-made cakes,
Fairtrade tea and coffee, served in the peaceful surroundings of
Helmsley Walled Garden. Open daily from 1st April to 31st October
10.30am-5pm.   C c w org
Chance Café ☎ 01482 446815
209 Chanterlands Avenue, Hull, East Yorkshire HU5 3TP   C L c w org
Hitchcock's Vegetarian Restaurant ☎ 01482 320233
1-2 Bishop Lane, Hull, East Yorkshire HU1 1PA   R L c
Zoo Café ☎ 01482 494352
80B Newland Avenue, Hull, East Yorkshire HU5 3AB   C c
Pollyanna's Tearoom ☎ 01423 869208
Jockey Lane, Knaresborough, North Yorkshire HG5 0HF   C L a
Hansa's Gujarati Vegetarian Restaurant ☎ 0113 244 4408
72/74 North Street, Leeds, West Yorkshire LS2 7PN
See display ad on page 64.   R L c org

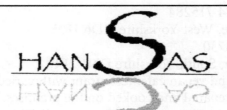
Little Tokyo ☎ 0113 243 9090
24 Central Road, Leeds, West Yorkshire LS1 6DE
Choice of tofu 'steak' dishes, vegan 'chicken' chunks, wild mushroom dishes; vegan and biodynamic wines served; home-made vegetarian sorbets.   R L a org

Roots & Fruits ☎ 0113 242 8313
10/11 Grand Arcade, Leeds, West Yorkshire LS1 6PG   C c

Airy Fairy ☎ 0114 249 2090
239 London Road, Sharrow, Sheffield, South Yorkshire S2 4NF
                                                                        C c w org

Blue Moon Café ☎ 0114 276 3443
2 St James Street, Sheffield, South Yorkshire S1 2EW   C L c w

The Fat Cat ☎ 0114 249 4801
23 Alma Street, Sheffield, South Yorkshire S3 8SA
Award-winning city pub, 150-year-old listed building. Beer garden.
Vegetarian and vegan dishes a speciality. Menu changes weekly.   P L a

'Homemade' ☎ 07774 013438
4 Netheredge Road, Sheffield, South Yorkshire S7 1RU
Home-made vegetarian and vegan food daily 9.30-4.30 except
Mondays. Also bistro-style evening bookings for 8-20 people with a 2
or 3 course menu.   C c

Nirmal Indian Tandoori ☎ 0114 272 4054
189-193 Glossop Road, Sheffield, South Yorkshire S10 2GW   R L a

Le Caveau Restaurant ☎ 01756 794274
86 High Street, Skipton, North Yorkshire BD23 1JJ   R L a

Wild Oats Café ☎ 01756 790619
10 High Street, Skipton, North Yorkshire BD23 1JZ   C b w

Dandelion and Burdock ☎ 01422 316000
16 Town Hall Street, Sowerby Bridge, West Yorkshire HX6 2EA
                                                            R L d org

The Magpie Café ☎ 01947 602058
14 Pier Road, Whitby, North Yorkshire YO21 3PU   R L a

The Blake Head Bookshop & Vegetarian Café ☎ 01904 623767
104 Micklegate, York YO1 6JX
Open 7 days a week serving breakfast, lunch and snacks. Child-
friendly and disabled access. All food home-made.   C L c w org

El Piano ☎ 01904 610676
15-17 Grape Lane, The Quarter, York YO1 7HU   R/C L d org

The Spurriergate Centre ☎ 01904 629393
St Michaels Church, Spurriergate, York YO1 9QR   C a

Cheshire

Cafés, restaurants, pubs

Hullabaloo ☎ 0161 941 4288
5 Kings Court, 39-40 Railway Street, Altrincham WA14 2RD
A 100% organic café serving high quality, freshly made sandwiches, salads, platters, soups and daily specials. Wonderful home-made cakes to boot! C a w org

Sokrates Greek Taverna ☎ 0161 282 0050
25A Northenden Road, Sale M33 2DH R L a org

Cumbria

Rothay Manor ☎ 015394 33605, fax 015394 33607
Rothay Bridge, Ambleside LA22 0EH

e-mail: hotel@rothaymanor.co.uk
website: www.rothaymanor.co.uk

Award-winning Country House Hotel in the heart of the Lake District. Ideal for walking, sightseeing or relaxing. Renowned for the warm, friendly atmosphere; excellent restaurant. Rooms and suites for families and disabled guests. Free use of nearby Leisure Centre. See also page 9.

H INS CatA L DA Ve NS Acc37

Barf House

☎ 017687 76789

Dubwath, Bassenthwaite Lake, Cockermouth CA13 9YD

e-mail: bob.pegasus@tiscali.co.uk
website: www.barfhouse.co.uk

Newly established 100% vegetarian accommodation in peaceful location near the shore of Bassenthwaite Lake. Magnificent views across to the Skiddaw range. Excellent base for walking, cycling, sailing or just relaxing. Evening meals and special diets available on request. Car & cycle parking.
GH CatB V Ve NS Acc4

Lancrigg Vegetarian Country House Hotel

☎ 015394 35317

Easedale, Grasmere LA22 9QN

e-mail: info@lancrigg.co.uk
website: www.lancrigg.co.uk

Peace and relaxation in historic country house with comfortable accommodation. Some rooms with whirlpool baths. International vegetarian cuisine. Special diets. Restaurant fully certified organic. Therapies and entry to country health spa available. Stunning mountain setting with 30 acres private grounds.
H INS CatA L V Ve NS Acc26

Ardrig Vegetarian Bed and Breakfast

☎ 01539 736879

144 Windermere Road, Kendal LA9 5EZ

e-mail: womacks@talktalk.net
website: www.ardrigvegetarian.com

Ardrig is a quiet, friendly home with clean comfortable rooms. Breakfast is vegetarian/vegan, fresh, filling, mostly Fairtrade, organic food. Kendal has restaurants, arts centre, cinemas, museums, shops and transport links to lakes and fells.
PH INS CatB V Ve NS Acc5

The Screes Hotel

☎ and fax 019467 26262

Nether Wasdale, Seascale CA20 1ET

e-mail: info@thescreesinnwasdale.com
website: www.thescreesinnwasdale.com

The Screes Inn is situated in the heart of Wasdale in the Lake District. We are a small family-run inn accommodating up to 12 people. Johnny, our vegetarian head chef, cooks a wide range of vegetarian and some vegan food.
H INS CatA L DA Ve NS CN Acc12

Hazel Bank Country House

☎ 017687 77248, fax 017687 77373

Rosthwaite, Borrowdale, Keswick CA12 5XB

e-mail: enquiries@hazelbankhotel.co.uk
website: www.hazelbankhotel.co.uk

Hazel Bank stands peacefully amidst 4-acre gardens with breathtaking views of Central Lakeland. Bedrooms are luxuriously furnished, well-proportioned, fully en-suite with stunning views. AA Red Rosette

for Fine Food, AA 5 Gold Stars (93% Merit Award score), VisitBritain 5 Stars + Gold Award, RAC Little Gem 2002-2006, RAC Two Dining Awards 2002-2006. Non-smoking. No pets.
G INS CatA L DA Ve NS Acc16

Nab Cottage
☎ 015394 35311, fax 015394 35493

Rydal, Ambleside LA22 9SD

e-mail: tim@nabcottage.com
website: www.rydalwater.com

In the heart of the Lake District, Nab Cottage is beautifully situated overlooking Rydal Water and surrounded by mountains. It dates from the 16th century and has many literary associations. Cosy, informal atmosphere - delicious home-cooked food. Shiatsu, massage and Reiki available. See also page 9.
G INS CatB Ve NS Acc18

Sefton House
☎ 01229 582190

34 Queen Street, Ulverston LA12 7AF

e-mail: reservations@seftonhouse.co.uk
website: www.seftonhouse.co.uk

Sefton House is a clean and comfortable family-run guest house, centrally located in the traditional market town of Ulverston. Our vegetarian breakfasts are freshly prepared using locally-grown, organic and Fairtrade ingredients wherever possible. We cater for special diets.
G INS CatB V Ve NS Acc11

St John's Lodge

☎ 015394 43078, fax 015394 88054

Lake Road, Windermere LA23 2EQ

e-mail: mail@st-johns-lodge.co.uk
website: www.st-johns-lodge.co.uk

See display ad below.
G INS CatB Ve NS CN Acc24

Cafés, restaurants, pubs

Siskins Café ☎ 017687 78410
  Whinlatter Visitor Centre, Braithwaite, Keswick CA12 5TW   C L a w org
Watermill Café ☎ 016974 78267
  Priests Mill, Caldbeck, Wigton CA7 8DR   C a org
Quince & Medlar Restaurant ☎ 01900 823579
  13 Castlegate, Cockermouth CA13 9EU   R L c

The Green Valley Organic Restaurant at Lancrigg ☎ 015394 35317
Easedale, Grasmere LA22 9QN
Fully organic. Healthy, delicious and nutritious. Special diets. All ingredients certified 100% organic. Open every day. Breakfasts, lunches, afternoon teas, evening meals. Stunning location, ½ mile from Grasmere village. Website www.greenvalleyorganic.co.uk and e-mail purefood@greenvalleyorganic.co.uk   R/C c w org

The Quaker Tapestry and Tearooms ☎ 01539 722975
Quaker Tapestry Exhibition Centre, Friends Meeting House, Stramongate, Kendal LA9 4BH
See display ad above.   C c

Union Jack Café ☎ 01539 722458
15 Kirkland, Kendal LA9 5AF   C L a

Waterside Wholefoods Café/Restaurant & Shop ☎ 01539 733252/729743
Kent View, Waterside, Kendal LA9 4DZ
See display ad on page 72.   C L c w org

The Lakeland Pedlar Wholefood Café ☎ 017687 74492
Hendersons Yard, Bell Close, Keswick CA12 5JD
See display ad on page 72.   R/C L c w org

Maysons Restaurant ☎ 017687 74104
  33 Lake Road, Keswick CA12 5DQ   R L a
Little Salkeld Watermill ☎ 01768 881523
  Little Salkeld, Penrith CA10 1NN
  The watermill tearoom famous for delicious food – bread, cakes,
  biscuits and pies from flour milled in Cumbria's traditional working
  watermill.   C c w org
The Village Bakery ☎ 01768 881811
  Melmerby, nr Penrith CA10 1HE
  Organic restaurant and bakeshop specialising in products suitable for
  people with special diet requirements. Open all year (excluding
  Christmas and New Year).   R/C L a w org

Isle of Man

Fernleigh   ☎ and fax 01624 842435
Marine Parade, Peel IM5 1PB

e-mail: fernleigh@manx.net
website: www.isleofman.com/accommodation/fernleigh

Looking across the bay, in the quiet fishing village of Peel. Join us in
our comfortable
Victorian home on
the sea front,
standard and en-
suite rooms.

PEEL CASTLE

Complemented by
our excellent choice of home-made vegetarian and traditional
breakfasts. Standard room £25.00, en-suite £30.00 p.p.p.n.
G INS CatB Ve NS Acc22

Cafés, restaurants, pubs
Greens Vegetarian Restaurant ☎ 01624 629129
  Steam Railway Station, Bank Hill, Douglas IM1 4LL   R/C L c

The Cameo

30 Hornby Road,
Blackpool FY1 4QG

Tel 01253 626144, fax 01253 296048

www.blackpool-cameo.com
enquiries@blackpool-cameo.com

The Cameo is a small, friendly guest house in
the popular central area of Blackpool. The
owners, Janet and Phil, are vegetarian and
offer clean comfortable accommodation for families, couples, small
groups of friends and individuals (with no single occupancy charges).
Special interest groups also welcome.

All our rooms are en-suite with TV/radio/alarm, unlimited tea/coffee-
making facilities and hairdryers.

Lancashire, Greater Manchester and Merseyside

The Cameo
☎ 01253 626144, fax 01253 296048

30 Hornby Road, Blackpool FY1 4QG

e-mail: enquiries@blackpool-cameo.com
website: www.blackpool-cameo.com

See display ad above
G INS CatC L Ve NS Acc20

Edendale House
☎ 01704 530718

83 Avondale Road North, Southport, Merseyside PR9 0NE

e-mail: edendalehouse@aol.com
website: www.edendalehouse.co.uk

Peace, tranquillity and a warm welcome await you at the Edendale

House, where we are proud to offer you warm friendly service in a relaxed comfortable atmosphere. All rooms en-suite. Off-road parking. Short stroll to town centre.

G INS CatB L NS Acc16

Cafés, restaurants, pubs

Vfresh Café ☎ 01254 844550

35 King Street, Blackburn BB2 2DH   C c

Red Triangle Café ☎ 01282 832319

160 St James Street, Burnley BB11 1NR

Just off Burnley town centre, we are an informal daytime café (Tuesday to Saturday) and a relaxed candlelit bistro for evening meals – Fridays, Saturdays and other evenings on request. We also provide buffets for events within travelling distance.   R/C L c

Jim's Café ☎ 01282 868828
19-21 New Market Street, Colne BB8 9BJ
Fresh seasonal food, using locally-sourced ingredients; served with high quality, affordable wines, in a creative, sensual, Parisian café environment.   R L c w org

Sokrates Greek Taverna ☎ 01204 692100
80-84 Winter Hey Lane, Horwich, Bolton BL6 7NZ   R L a org

Everyman @ Blackwell's ☎ 0151 709 0025
Blackwell University Bookshop, University of Liverpool, Alsop Building, Brownlow Hill, Liverpool L3 5TX
See display ad on page 75.   C a org

Everyman Bistro and Bars ☎ 0151 708 9545
5-9 Hope Street, Liverpool L1 9BH   R L a w org

Greenfish Café ☎ 0151 707 8592
11 Upper Newington, Liverpool L1 2SR   C c

The Piazza Café Bar ☎ 0151 707 3536
The Metropolitan Cathedral, Mount Pleasant, Liverpool L3 5QX
See display ad on page 77.   C L a org

Earth Vegetarian Café and Juice Bar ☎ 0161 834 1996
16-20 Turner Street, Northern Quarter, Manchester M4 1DZ
10-7 Tuesday-Friday, 10-5 Saturday. Award-winning café with fresh, seasonal home cooking. Fairtrade, vegan, ethical food, juices, drinks and cakes.   C d

Everyman @ Blackwell's ☎ 0161 273 8000
Blackwell University Bookshop, The Precinct Centre, Oxford Road, Manchester M13 9RN
See display ad on page 75.   C a org

On the Eighth Day Vegetarian Health Food Shop and Café
☎ 0161 273 1850
111 Oxford Road, Manchester M1 7DU   C L c w

duk ☎ 01772 202220
16-18 Lancaster Road, Preston PR1 1DA   R L a w org

Ramsons ☎ 01706 825070
16-18 Market Place, Ramsbottom BL0 9HT   R L a org

the piazza

- Menu changes daily
- Delicious main meals
- Stupendous soups & salads
- Incredible sandwiches & cakes
- Veggie & gluten-free options
- Wines, beers & spirits

The Piazza Café Bar at the Metropolitan Cathedral has new opening hours, a new menu and new proprietor - Alan Crowe, ex General Manager of the Everyman Bistro.

We'll be open: 8.00am - 5.00pm initially, extending to 8.00pm in December. Car parking at rear. We look forward to seeing you soon...

FIERCELY FRESH FOOD

CAFE BAR FOOD TO GO

Wales

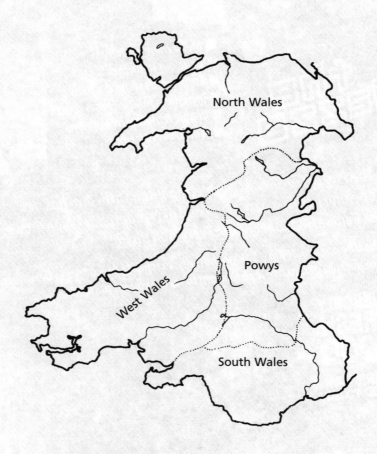

North Wales

Powys

West Wales

South Wales

North Wales

Bronwen Cottage
☎ 01248 450533

Rhoscefnhir, Pentraeth, Anglesey LL75 8YS

e-mail: ulrike@schade.fsnet.co.uk
website: www.bronwenlivingfoods.co.uk

A peaceful family-run B&B. Food served is of high quality, mainly organic, using home-grown and local produce. Purified water is also used. We are partially powered by solar and run our van on waste vegetable oil. See also page 9.
PH CatB Ve NS CN Acc2

Bodnant Guest House
☎ 01492 876936

39 St Mary's Road, Llandudno, Conwy LL30 2UE

e-mail: dyfrig.williams@talk21.com
website: www.bodnantguesthouse.biz

Bodnant is a beautiful, Victorian, 4 Star guest house with many original features, where limited numbers ensure warm, personal, friendly service. We are situated only a couple of minutes' walk from beach and promenade and all amenities.
G INS CatB NS Acc12

Ivy House
☎ 01341 422535, fax 01341 422689

Finsbury Square, Dolgellau, Gwynedd LL40 1RF

e-mail: marg.bamford@btconnect.com
website: www.ivyhouse-dolgellau.co.uk

Country town guest house offering attractive accommodation, good food and a welcoming atmosphere. The six bedrooms have TV, hairdryers and tea/coffee facilities, four of them have en-suite facilities. Delicious vegetarian/traditional breakfasts and evening meals. Open all year.
G INS CatB Ve NS Acc13

Graianfryn

☎ 01286 871007

Penisarwaun, Caernarfon, Gwynedd LL55 3NH

e-mail: christine@fastasleep.me.uk
website: www.fastasleep.me.uk

Set in beautiful countryside between mountains and seas, Graianfryn offers exclusively vegetarian/vegan delicious gourmet meals including home-made bread, cereals, ice-cream etc. Only 3 miles from Snowdon, enjoy wonderful walks, lovely beaches, castles, burial chambers and more.
G CatB L V Ve NS Acc6

Tremeifion Vegetarian Hotel

☎ 01766 770491

Soar Road, Talsarnau, nr Harlech, Gwynedd LL47 6UH

e-mail: enquire@tremeifionvegetarianhotel.co.uk
website: www.tremeifionvegetarianhotel.co.uk

See display ad on page 80.
H CatA L V Ve NS CN Acc10

Cafés, restaurants, pubs

Alpine Coffee Shop and Gallery ☎ 01690 710747
  Station Approach, Betws-y-Coed, Conwy LL24 0AE   C a
Beddgelert Tearooms & Bistro ☎ 01766 890543
  Waterloo House, Beddgelert, Gwynedd LL55 4UY   R L a

Powys

Trericket Mill Vegetarian Guest House, Bunkhouse & Camping ☎ 01982 560312
Erwood, Builth Wells LD2 3TQ

e-mail: mail@trericket.co.uk
website: www.trericket.co.uk

We offer a range of accommodation overlooking the River Wye, from camping and bunkroom, with optional bedding and breakfast, to en-suite bed and wholesome vegetarian breakfast in our grade 2* listed corn mill and cosy bunkhouse set in an old cider orchard beside the mill stream. Small but friendly! Contact Nicky or Alistair Legge.
G INS CatB V Ve NS Acc16+camping

Elan Valley Hotel   ☎ 01597 810448, fax 01597 810824
Elan Valley, nr Rhayader LD6 5HN
e-mail: info@elanvalleyhotel.co.uk
website: www.elanvalleyhotel.co.uk
See display ad below and also page 11.
H INS CatA L DA Ve NS Acc20+

Primrose Earth Retreats   ☎ 01497 847636
Primrose Farm, Felindre, Brecon LD3 0ST
e-mail: jan.benham@ukonline.co.uk
website: www.primroseearthcentre.co.uk
Organic fruit and vegetable smallholding at the foot of the Black Mountains; on national cycle route; near Hay-on-Wye. Guests prepare own breakfast, we provide fresh ingredients. B&B, evening meals on request; quiet retreats for de-stressing from busy lives; sound healing courses available.
PH CatC V Ve NS CN Acc5

The Old Post Office

Llanigon, **Hay-on-Wye** HR3 5QA

Tel 01497 820008

website: www.oldpost-office.co.uk

Exclusively vegetarian

A very special find at the foot of the
Black Mountains and **only two miles from the famous second-hand book
town of Hay-on-Wye**.

Charming 17th-century house with beams and oak floor boards. Lovely walks
and views of the Wye Valley and Black Mountains. Dogs by arrangement.
Rough Guide, Lonely Planet, Alastair Sawday's *Special Places to Stay* and *Which?*
recommended.

We also have a Georgian cottage in Hay-on-Wye available as holiday let or
B&B (self-serve continental breakfast).

Please visit our website for more information.

The Old Post Office   ☎ 01497 820008

Llanigon, Hay-on-Wye HR3 5QA

website: www.oldpost-office.co.uk

See display ad above.
G CatB V Ve NS CN Acc6

Cafés, restaurants, pubs

The Quarry Café ☎ 01654 702624

  13 Heol Maengwyn, Machynlleth SY20 8EB   C c w org

The Hat Shop Restaurant ☎ 01544 260017

  7 High Street, Presteigne LD8 2BA   R L a w org

Old Swan Tea Rooms & Cake Shop ☎ 01597 811060

  West Street, Rhayader LD6 5AB   C a

South Wales
Awen Vegetarian B&B and Dining

☎ 01495 244615

Penrhiwgwair Cottage, Twyn Road, Abercarn, Newport, Gwent NP11 5AS

e-mail: info@awenbandb.com
website: www.awenbandb.com

Our award-winning, exclusively vegetarian, environmentally-friendly B&B now offers seasonal organic dining. This historic 16th-century cottage has a romantic four-poster bed and many original features.
Breathtaking scenery and mountain walks outside the front door. Vegan and special diets welcomed. See also page 11.

G CatB V Ve NS Acc6

Cafés, restaurants, pubs

Hunky Dory's Vegetarian Restaurant ☎ 01633 257850
   17 Charles Street, Newport, Gwent NP20 1JU   R c w org
Caffi Bar Chapter ☎ 02920 304400
   Chapter Arts Centre, Market Road, Canton, Cardiff, South Glamorgan CF5 1QE
   Always fresh, always seasonal, at Chapter you'll find lovingly cooked, mouth-watering food in a fun and friendly arts centre atmosphere.
C L a org

Crumbs ☎ 02920 395007
   33 Morgan Arcade, Cardiff, South Glamorgan CF10 1AF
   DO YOUR BODY A FAVOUR – EAT 'CRUMBS'! Established 1970 by present proprietor Judi. Home-made salads and hot food. All veggie – some vegan, wheat- and dairy-free.   R c
Embassy Café ☎ 02920 373144
   Cathays Community Centre, 36 Cathays Terrace, Cardiff, South Glamorgan CF24 4HX   C a org

Vegetarian Food Studio ☎ 02920 238222
  109 Penarth Road, Cardiff, South Glamorgan CF11 6JT   R/C c
Govinda's Vegetarian Restaurant ☎ 01792 468469
  8 Cradock Street, Swansea, West Glamorgan SA1 3EN
  See display ad above.   R c org

West Wales

Heartspring
☎ 01267 241999

Hill House, Llansteffan, nr Carmarthen, Carmarthenshire SA33 5JG

e-mail: info@heartspring.co.uk
website: www.heartspring.co.uk

Magical Retreat Centre superbly situated overlooking a stunning coastal conservation area. Exclusively vegan/vegetarian and 100% organic with our own spring water, and no smoking throughout. We offer retreats (not aligned to any religion) and self-contained apartments for peaceful and healing holidays with the option of nurturing sessions with our team of professional complementary practitioners. See also page 11.
Retreat Centre CatA V Ve NS Acc14

Rhyd-y-Groes B&B
☎ and fax 01570 470188

Bwlchllan, Lampeter, Ceredigion SA48 8QN

e-mail: enquiries@rhyd-y-groes.com
website: www.rhyd-y-groes.com

Peaceful 4 Star accommodation in rural setting with panoramic views of surrounding countryside, easily accessible from the B4337. Hot Tub/Spa, aromatherapy available. Convenient base for relaxing or activity breaks. Local wildlife includes red kites, dolphins and seals. Enjoy an evening meal in the newly renovated restaurant, seasonal alfresco dining and BBQs in restaurant garden. Vegetarian menu, speciality home-baked bread, fresh duck eggs when laying. Special diets catered for. Vegetarian Society accredited, bronze Welsh Food Hygiene Award. Equine B&B also available.
PH INS CatB Ve NS CN Acc8

Over the Rainbow

☎ 01239 811155

Plas Tyllwyd, Tanygroes, nr Cardigan, Ceredigion SA43 2JD

e-mail: info@overtherainbowwales.co.uk
website: www.overtherainbowwales.co.uk

See display ad above and also page 11.
G CatB V Ve NS CN Acc9

Cuffern Manor

☎ 01437 710071

Roch, Haverfordwest, Pembrokeshire SA62 6HB

e-mail: enquiries@cuffernmanor.co.uk
website: www.cuffernmanor.co.uk

Our eighteenth-century Manor House
in the spectacular Pembrokeshire
countryside is adjacent to the stunning

Pembrokeshire Coast National Park near Newgale Beach. Wifi access. Lift and accessible shower/toilet. Quality organic, fair-traded food or local produce. Delicious vegetarian and vegan food. Winner of Pembrokeshire Produce 2006 Award for 'Best use of local food'. See also page 11.

G INS CatB DA Ve NS CN Acc20

Cafés, restaurants, pubs

Waverley Vegetarian Restaurant ☎ 01267 236521
23 Lammas Street, Carmarthen, Carmarthenshire SA31 3AL

R L c w org

The Hive on the Quay ☎ 01545 570445
Cadwgan Place, Aberaeron, Ceredigion SA46 0BU   R/C L a

The Treehouse ☎ 01970 615791
14 Stryd y Popty/Baker Street, Aberystwyth, Ceredigion SY23 2BJ
Aberystwyth's favourite café and shop for the best organic, local and seasonal produce. Vegans, vegetarians, carnivores and free-thinkers all welcome.   C L a w org

The Mulberry Bush ☎ 01570 423317
2 Bridge Street, Lampeter, Ceredigion SA48 7HG   C L c w org

The Refectory at St Davids
St Davids Cathedral, St Davids, Haverfordwest, Pembrokeshire SA62 6RH   C L a

Scotland

Orkney and Shetland Islands (NE of the Scottish mainland, here shown at half scale of main map)

Western Scottish Islands

Scottish Highlands

Aberdeenshire and Moray

Angus, Perth and Kinross

Argyll

Fife

Central Scotland

Lothian

Ayrshire

Borders

Dumfries and Galloway

Aberdeenshire & Moray

Fournet House Accommodation

☎ 01340 821428

Balvenie Street, Dufftown, Moray AB55 4AB

e-mail: alison@woosnam8488.freeserve.co.uk
website: www.noahsarkbistro.co.uk

Fournet House provides a haven in the hills in Dufftown in North East Scotland for 'Wellbeing at its Best'. Located halfway between the beautiful scenic coast and the Braes of Glenlivet and the Cabrach, it is easily accessible from either Inverness or Aberdeen airports. Come by train to Huntly or Keith station or bring your own car! On offer is outrageously comfortable accommodation en-suite and one bedroom has its own foaming whirlpool bath. Feel at home in the lovely reception room. There is a variety of things to do and delicious and innovative food to enjoy. The wellbeing and therapy garden is being developed at the back of the house. Choose from a collection of packages or simply taste the experience in an overnight stay. Please watch the website for more details. See also page 12.
G CatB L Ve NS Acc6

Allandale Cottage

☎ 01343 842052

Main Street, Urquhart, nr Elgin, Moray IV30 8LG

e-mail: dinniebrooks@yahoo.co.uk
website: www.allandalecottage.co.uk

Small, friendly B&B in traditional Scottish cottage. Guest lounge with open fire. Delicious continental breakfasts, brought to your room if preferred. We're a vegetarian household and also cater for vegans. Dolphin watching, Findhorn Foundation, lovely walks and cycle routes nearby.
PH CatC V Ve NS Acc2

Cafés, restaurants, pubs

Noah's Ark Whole Food Café and Licensed Bistro ☎ 01340 821428
Fournet House, Balvenie Street, Dufftown, Moray AB55 4AB
Fun, funky and irrepressible! The handmade, whole food cuisine is
served from breakfast through to delicious dinner. Noah's Ark offers a
wide nutritional rainbow on a plate, including new in 2009, its own
home-grown vegetables complementing the locally sourced produce.

R/C L a w

Argyll

White Rock Bed & Breakfast ☎ 01546 870310
Leac Na Ban, Tayvallich, nr Lochgilphead PA31 8PF

e-mail: whiterock.argyll@btinternet.com
website: whiterock-argyll.co.uk

In our hilltop farmhouse we provide comfortable accommodation,
good vegetarian/vegan food, and the peace and quiet of this lovely
part of Scotland. Substantial evening meals (and picnics) by
arrangement, using home-grown and organic local produce whenever
possible. See also page 12.
PH CatC Ve NS CN Acc4

Cafés, restaurants, pubs

The Smiddy Bistro ☎ 01546 603606
Smithy Lane, Lochgilphead PA31 8TA   R L a

Ayrshire

Drumskeoch Farm B&B ☎ 01465 841172
Pinwherry, nr Girvan KA26 0QB

e-mail: drumskeoch@wildmail.com
website: www.drumskeoch.co.uk
Unique family-run green, organic
vegetarian/vegan B&B in naturally renovated
rural farmhouse, with own water source and
beautiful views of the surrounding hills.
Comfortable and relaxed atmosphere,
delicious home-cooked food, and a great base
for walking, sightseeing or relaxing.
PH CatB V Ve NS CN Acc4

Borders

Cafés, restaurants, pubs

Tibbie Shiels Inn ☎ 01750 42231
St Mary's Loch, Selkirkshire, Scottish Borders TD7 5LH
We have a choice of vegetarian meals and will accommodate dietary
requirements from coeliacs to vegans on request. This historic coaching
inn is located 16 miles from Selkirk, on the A708 to Moffat.   R/P L a

Dumfries and Galloway

Cafés, restaurants, pubs

Abbey Cottage ☎ 01387 850377
26 Main Street, New Abbey, Dumfries DG2 8BY
Situated beside historical Sweetheart Abbey, we serve morning coffee,
light lunches and afternoon tea, baked or cooked on our premises.
Also gift shop stocking preserves and crafts from around the region.
www.abbeycottagetearoom.com   R L a w org

Edinburgh

Ardgarth Guest House

☎ 0131 669 3021, fax 0131 468 1221

1 St Mary's Place, Portobello, Edinburgh EH15 2QF

e-mail: stay@ardgarth.com
website: www.ardgarth.com

Tastefully adapted from a large
Victorian home, in a wide, quiet
street with easy parking. City centre
20 minutes by bus, short stroll to
sandy beach and a promenade that
is the envy of Edinburgh! Single,
double, twin and family rooms,
some en-suite. Cots/high chairs
available. Ground floor rooms fully equipped for disabled people.
G INS CatB L DA Ve NS Acc21

Elmview

☎ 0131 228 1973

15 Glengyle Terace, Edinburgh EH3 9LN

e-mail: nici@elmview.co.uk
website: www.elmview.co.uk

Robin and Nici Hill's elegant and
peaceful accommodation is situated in
the heart of Edinburgh, only 15 minutes'
walk from Princes Street and Edinburgh
Castle. Totally non-smoking and graded
5 Stars by the AA.
PH INS CatA Ve NS Acc8

Six Mary's Place Guest House

☎ 0131 332 8965, fax 0131 624 7060

Raeburn Place, Stockbridge, Edinburgh EH4 1JH

e-mail: info@sixmarysplace.co.uk
website: www.sixmarysplace.co.uk

See display ad below.
G INS CatA V Ve NS Acc23

The Walton

☎ 0131 556 1137, fax 0131 557 8367

79 Dundas Street, Edinburgh EH3 6SD

e-mail: enquiries@waltonhotel.com
website: www.waltonhotel.com

See display ad on page 95.
G INS CatA NS Acc24

Cafés, restaurants, pubs

Ann Purna Vegetarian Indian Restaurant ☎ 0131 662 1807
44 St Patricks Square, Edinburgh EH8 9ET
The finest Indian Gujarati cuisine in town. We offer traditional home-style Indian cooking set in a friendly atmosphere with excellent service. R L c

The Baked Potato Shop ☎ 0131 225 7572
56 Cockburn Street, Edinburgh EH1 1PB
Extensive selection of vegetarian/vegan fillings, plus vegan cakes home made. Open 7 days 9am-9pm. Take-away c

Cornerstone Café ☎ 0131 229 0212
Under St John's Church, 1 Lothian Road, Edinburgh EH2 4BJ
C L a org

David Bann Restaurant ☎ 0131 556 5888
56-58 St Mary's Street, Edinburgh EH1 1SX R L c

The Engine Shed ☎ 0131 662 0040
19 St Leonard's Lane, Edinburgh EH8 9SD
See display ad on page 96. R/C c org

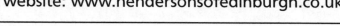

Filmhouse Café Bar ☎ 0131 229 5932
88 Lothian Road, Edinburgh EH3 9BZ C L a w org
Henderson's Bistro ☎ 0131 225 2605
25 Thistle Street, Edinburgh EH2 1DR R L c w org
Henderson's Salad Table ☎ 0131 225 2131
94 Hanover Street, Edinburgh EH2 1DR
See display ad on page 96. R L c w org
Henderson's Wine Bar ☎ 0131 225 2131
94 Hanover Street, Edinburgh EH2 1DR Wine bar L c w org

Glasgow and Central Scotland

Adelaide's ☎ 0141 248 4970, fax 0141 226 4247
209 Bath Street, Glasgow G2 4HZ

e-mail: reservations@adelaides.co.uk
website: www.adelaides.co.uk

Highly acclaimed Guest House situated in

award-winning listed building with family/twin/double and single en-suites available. Our friendly, knowledgeable staff make Adelaide's *the* ideal base from which to explore Glasgow, The Friendly City.
G INS CatA Ve NS Acc20

Cafés, restaurants, pubs

Grassroots Café ☎ 0141 333 0534
  93-97 St George's Road, Charing Cross, Glasgow G3 6JA
  Innovative vegetarian and vegan food served in laid-back Bohemian surroundings. Freshly baked organic cakes and delicious organic coffee. Open 7 days a week. C L c org

mono ☎ 0141 553 2400
  12 Kings Court, King Street, Glasgow G1 5RB
  Exciting café/bar in Glasgow's Merchant City. All our tasty food is animal-free. Site includes microbrewery/venue/gallery/record shop. Website www.monocafebar.com. See display ad on page 97.
  C/P L d w org

STEREO ☎ 0141 222 2254

20-28 Renfield Lane, Glasgow G2 6PH
City centre café/bar near Central Station. Breads, pies, cakes baked on premises. Healthy sit-in or take-away. Delicious salads and coffee. Website www.stereocafebar.com. See display ad on page 98.

C/P L d w org

Tapa Coffee & Bakehouse ☎ 0141 554 9981

19-21 Whitehill Street, Dennistoun, Glasgow G31 2LH
Tapa is an organic bakery, coffee roasterie & café. Everything is made on the premises using fresh, organic ingredients. Open 7 days.

C c w org

The 78 ☎ 0141 576 5018

14 Kelvinhaugh Street, Glasgow G3 8NU
Delightful pub in west end of Glasgow serving delicious and healthy animal-free food. Organic drinks, real fire, 1927 gramophone! Website www.the78cafebar.com. See display ad above.

C/P L d w org

Creag Meagaidh B&B

☎ 01540 673798, fax 0870 838 1101

Main Street, Newtonmore, Inverness-shire PH20 1DP

e-mail: creag-meagaidh@live.co.uk
website: www.creag-meagaidh.co.uk

Luxurious B&B within Cairngorm National Park. Mountains, lochs and rivers all within walking distance. Home-made bread and jams, Fairtrade tea and coffee. Full board available for groups/longer stays. Vegetarian owners. Close to train and bus stops. See also page 12.
PH INS CatB Ve NS Acc6

Cuildorag House

☎ 01855 821529

Onich, nr Fort William, Inverness-shire PH33 6SD

e-mail: enquiries@cuildoraghouse.com
website: www.cuildoraghouse.com

Stay and relax in our comfortable Victorian house set amongst spectacular lochs and mountains. Large delicious breakfasts and evening meals (often organic and from the garden). Days walking, mountain biking, touring, exploring Ben Nevis, Glencoe, Ardnamurchan, castles, steam trains …

PH CatB V Ve NS Acc6

Woodland ☎ 01549 441715
Rosehall, by Lairg, Sutherland IV27 4BD

e-mail: mail@vegetarian-scotland.com
website: www.vegetarian-scotland.com

Woodland is a vegetarian B&B
and yoga retreat. Exclusively
vegetarian evening meals (vegan)
available by request. Yoga
holidays avalaible
(www.yogaretreatuk.co.uk).
Woodland in north-central
Scotland is the perfect base to
explore the Highlands. Go
walking here in some of the nicest
scenery in the UK.
PH INS CatB DA V Ve NS CN Acc6

Cafés, restaurants, pubs

Cawdor Castle ☎ 01667 404401
  Nairn, Inverness-shire IV12 5RD
                    R L a org (open 1st May to 2nd Sunday in October)
Station Tea Room and Craft Shop ☎ 01349 865894
  Station Square, Dingwall, Ross-shire IV15 9JX   C a
The Ceilidh Place ☎ 01854 612103
  14 West Argyle Street, Ullapool, Ross-shire IV26 2TY
                                        R/C/P L a w org
Loch Croispol Bookshop & Restaurant ☎ 01971 511777
  2 Balnakeil Craft Village, Durness, by Lairg, Sutherland IV27 4PT
                                        R L a

Shetland Islands

Cafés, restaurants, pubs

Da Böd Café ☎ 01806 503348

Hillswick Wildlife Sanctuary, Hillswick ZE2 9RW

We serve vegetarian and vegan food in a 400-year-old building. Open May to September from 11am, please phone to book an evening meal. Payment by donation. Also B&B for 2 people in a lovely room with sea views. All proceeds go to Hillswick Wildlife Sanctuary, a seal and otter sanctuary.

C c w org

The Western Scottish Islands

The Old Croft House Vegetarian B&B

☎ 01470 532375

6 Carbost, Skeabost Bridge, by Portree, Isle of Skye IV51 9PD

e-mail: samcrowe@tiscali.co.uk
website: www.vegetarianskye.co.uk

Come for a relaxing stay in our beautiful 19th-century croft house. We aim to provide a B&B experience that is a bit special, with stunning views, breakfasts that are truly indulgent and great hosts, who will really look after you.

PH CatB V Ve NS CN Acc2+child

Foxwood

Foxwood is surrounded by inspirational countryside, standing in 4 acres of land with sea and mountain views. The sunrises and sunsets can be unbelievable.

Spacious en-suites, and single room.

Sauna, jacuzzi, steam cabinet and alternative therapies are available.

Ideal for touring, walking, cycling, relaxing.

11a Ullinish by Struan, Isle of Skye IV56 8FD

e-mail treefox@hotmail.com
website www.scotland-info.co.uk/foxwood

NOMINATED
Customer Excellence Award
2008

JJ's
Bistro
01470
572782

Gourmet
Society

Struan, Isle of Skye

www.jjsbistro-skye.com

Incorporating an extensive vegetarian menu

Special diets catered for with prior arrangement
Booking advisable but not essential

We look forward to welcoming you

Foxwood
☎ 01470 572331

11A Ullinish by Struan, Isle of Skye IV56 8FD

e-mail: treefox@hotmail.com
website: www.scotland-info.co.uk/foxwood

See display ad on page 103.
G CatB DA V Ve NS CN Acc6

Cafés, restaurants, pubs

JJ's Bistro   ☎ 01470 572782
  Struan, Isle of Skye IV56 8FB
  See display ad on page 103.   R L a org

Further vegetarian information

For users of this guide who would like further information on vegetarianism or veganism in Britain, or information on a particular area, we list below a number of organisations, groups and information centres. When writing, please include a stamp for return postage.

National

Friends Vegetarian Society
9 Astons Close, Woods Lane, Amblecote, nr Stourbridge, West Midlands DY5 2QT, tel 01384 423899

Jewish Vegetarian Society
855 Finchley Road, London NW11 8LX, tel 020 8455 0692

Muslim Vegan/Vegetarian Society
59 Bray Towers, 136 Adelaide Road, London NW3 3JU, tel 020 7483 1742
Run by Rafeeque Ahmed, who has written a booklet called 'Islam and Vegetarianism' which is available at £1.

The Vegetarian Society (UK) Ltd.
Parkdale, Dunham Road, Altrincham, Cheshire WA14 4QG, tel 0161 925 2000, fax 0161 926 9182

The Vegan Society Ltd.
21 Hylton Street, Hockley, Birmingham B18 6HJ, tel 0845 458 8244/0121 523 1730

Viva! (Vegetarians International Voice for Animals)
8 York Court, Wilder Street, Bristol BS2 8QH, tel 0845 456 8220, fax 0845 456 8230
Viva! actively and successfully campaigns to stop cruelty to animals and to promote a vegetarian/vegan lifestyle. Free information available from the above address.

Young Indian Vegetarians
226 London Road, West Croydon, Surrey CR0 2TF, e-mail animalahimsa@yahoo.co.uk

England (by county)

Bedfordshire Vegetarians
The Old Spinney, 69 The Ridgeway, Flitwick, Bedfordshire MK45 1DJ, e-mail bunnymunch@hotmail.com

Bedford Veggies & Vegans
Tel 01234 741253, e-mail greenkatgreen@hotmail.co.uk

Thames Valley Vegans & Vegetarians
68 Peppard Road, Emmer Green, Reading, Berkshire RG4 8TL, tel 0118 946 4858, e-mail t3v@makessense.co.uk

Chiltern Veggies
7 Bedford Avenue, Amersham, Buckinghamshire HP6 6PT, tel 01753 893069, e-mail chilternveggies@yahoo.co.uk

Milton Keynes Vegetarians & Vegans
13 Peers Lane, Shenley Church End, Milton Keynes, Buckinghamshire MK5 6BG, tel 01908 503919, e-mail mkvegan475@talktalk.net

Peterborough Vegetarian Group
28 Glendale, Orton Wistow, Peterborough, Cambridgeshire PE2 6YL, tel 01733 230314, e-mail pboroveggies@hotmail.co.uk

Chester & Clwyd Vegetarian Group
Nant Yr Hafod Cottage, Hafod
Bilston, Llandegla, Clwyd LL11 3BG,
tel 01978 790442, e-mail
indesigneko@aol.com

Chester Vegetarians and Vegans
7 Foxwist Close, Chester, Cheshire
CH2 2DS, tel 07962 285213, e-mail
chesterveg@hotmail.co.uk

Stockport Vegetarians and Vegans
(Cheshire) tel 0161 217 9094, e-mail
antonybyatt@hotmail.com

Tees Valley Veggies & Vegans
3 Church Lane, Marske by the Sea,
Redcar TS11 7LJ, tel 07950 017928, e-
mail tees_veg@yahoo.co.uk

Newquay Veg Info Centre (Cornwall)
tel 01637 876987, e-mail
katie@wise.myzen.co.uk

Lakeland Living Veg Group
5 Bridge Street Close, Cockermouth,
Cumbria CA13 9RR, tel 01900
824045, e-mail
veggielakelandliving@tiscali.co.uk

Amber Valley Vegetarians & Vegans
(Derbyshire)
Tel 01773 833294, e-mail
amberveg@hotmail.co.uk

Derby Vegetarian Society
P.O. Box 41, Derby DE1 9ZR, tel 0871
855 3912, e-mail
manjit01@ntlworld.com

Derbyshire Vegetarians
tel 01298 72472

Dartveggie (Dartmouth, Devon, area)
e-mail dartveggie@hotmail.co.uk

Exeter Vision Info Centre
1 Romsey Drive, Exeter, Devon EX2
4PB, tel 01392 273694, e-mail
pace@eclipse.co.uk

North & Mid Devon Info Centre
Fern Tor, Meshaw, South Molton,
Devon EX36 4NA, tel 01769 550339,
e-mail veg@ferntor.co.uk

Plymouth Environment Centre
Greenbank Neighbourhood Office, 35
Armada Street, Plymouth, Devon PL4
8LZ, tel 01752 290015, e-mail
info@plymouthenvironmentcentre.co.uk
(Chris Deacon)

Dorset Vegans
Tel 01202 824783, e-mail
jjnanaz@yahoo.co.uk

Barking Vegetarian Info Centre
288 Howard Road, Barking, Essex
IG11 7DN, tel 020 8252 5846 evenings

North East Essex Vegetarian Information
tel 01206 263545, e-mail
APWh@aol.com

Southend Animal Aid
PO Box 211, Short Street, Southend on
Sea, Essex SS1 1AA, tel 01268 756026,
e-mail
southendanimalaid@hotmail.com

Southend Area Veggies (Essex)
tel 01702 540903, e-mail
soocoleman4@aol.com

VegSX
4 Tyrrells Road, Billericay, Essex
CM11 2QE, tel 07970 732668, e-mail
veganessex@hotmail.com

Manchester Vegan Society
69 Lonsdale Road, Heaton, Bolton
BL1 4PW, tel 07980 161025. e-mail
sarahalliez@yahoo.co.uk, website
www.manchester.vegangroup.co.uk

Manchester Vegetarian & Vegan Group
550 St Helens Road, Bolton BL3 3SJ,
tel 01204 654401, e-mail
mike@mvvg.co.uk

Vegetarian Information
  100 Sarah Robinson House, Queen
  Street, Portsmouth, Hampshire PO1
  3JA, e-mail
  michael.maybury2@ntlworld.com
Solent Vegetarians & Vegans (Hampshire)
  tel 023 8064 3813, e-mail
  info@solentveg.org.uk
Wye Valley Veggies
  3 New Street, Ledgemoor, Hereford
  HR4 8TA, tel 01432 277493, e-mail
  info@w-v-v.org.uk
North Herts Vegetarians and Vegans
  4 Oaktree Close, Letchworth Garden
  City, Hertfordshire SG6 3XY, tel 01462
  643424, e-mail
  info@nhvegetariansandvegans.org.uk
Isle of Wight Vegetarians
  Keepers Lock, Youngwood Way,
  Alverstone Garden Village, Sandown,
  Isle of Wight PO36 0HF, tel 01983
  407098, e-mail johnvl@tiscali.co.uk
Bexleyheath & Erith Vegetarian Info
  Centre (Kent)
  tel 01322 402713, mobile 07986
  670470
Bromley Eating Experience
  241 Pickhurst Rise, West Wickham,
  Kent BR4 0AH, tel 020 8777 1680
Canterbury & Coastal Veg Info Centre
  83 Cherry Gardens, Herne Bay, Kent
  CT6 5QY, tel 01227 375661
Medway Veggies & Vegans
  7 Masefield Drive, Cliffe Woods,
  Rochester, Kent ME3 8JW, tel 01634
  294865, e-mail
  sheilamccrossan@hotmal.com
North Kent Vegetarian Info Centre
  Sycamore Lodge, 71 Barton Hill Drive,
  Minster on Sea, Sheerness, Kent ME12

3NF, tel 01795 873987
Sevenoaks Vegetarians, Vegans and Fellow
  Travellers
  Westmount, Orchard Road, Pratts
  Bottom, Orpington, Kent BR6 7NT, tel
  01689 859716, e-mail
  lionden1@btinternet.com
Tunbridge Wells Vegan & Vegetarian
  Group (Kent)
  Fletchers Cottage, Knowle Lane,
  Halland BN8 6PR, tel 01825 841104,
  e-mail mark.hanna@virgin.net
Lancs Veg
  tel 01772 787163, e-mail
  heena.dave@virgin.net
Wellbeing Workshops Veg Info Centre
  PO Box 494, Bolton, Lancashire BL3
  1XP, tel 01204 704600, e-mail
  alwynne@wellbeingworkshopsworldwi
  de.com
Leicestershire Vegetarian and Vegan
  Group
  Beeches, Smeeton Road, Saddington,
  Leicestershire LE8 0QT, tel 07786
  175445, e-mail
  leicesterveggies@isd.co.uk
Grantham VegSoc
  3 Lindisfarne Way, Barrowby Lodge,
  Grantham, Lincolnshire NG31 8ST, tel
  07988 724773, e-mail
  granthamvegsoc@hotmail.co.uk
Grimsby Vegetarians
  Flat 3, 6 Regent Gardens, Grimsby,
  Lincolnshire DN34 5AT, tel 01472
  870738, e-mail
  gy.vegetarians@btinternet.com
Lincoln Vegetarians & Vegans Group and
  Info Centre
  tel 01522 576441, e-mail
  ros.7spireview@virgin.net

Louth Vegetarian Group
37 Church Lane, Manby, Lincolnshire
LN11 8HL, tel 01507 327687

Ealing Veggie Group (London)
e-mail ealingveg@yahoo.co.uk

Lesbian Vegans (London)
e-mail tiger@tiger3.plus.com

North West London Vegetarian Group
3 St David Close, Cowley UB8 3SE, tel
01895 441881, e-mail
chetna_jayjit@yahoo.com

South West London Veg Info Centre
Flat 424, Brandenburgh House, 116
Fulham Palace Road, London W6
9HH, tel 020 8741 6793, e-mail
swveg1@yahoo.co.uk

Merseyside Vegetarian Helplink
38 Hyacinth Close, Haydock, St
Helens, Merseyside WA11 0NZ, tel
01942 271761, e-mail
marg4646@hotmail.com

ScouseVeg
tel 0151 933 1338, e-mail
jane@vegsoc.org

Harrow Vegetarian Society
152 Kenton Road, Harrow, Middlesex
HA3 8AZ, tel 020 8907 1235, e-mail
kjoshi@pradipsweet.co.uk

Norfolk Vegetarian & Vegan Society
13 Ipswich Grove, Norwich, Norfolk
NR2 2LU, tel 01603 620784, e-mail
aliciahowell@btinternet.com

West Norfolk Veggies
e-mail wnveggies@hotmail.co.uk

Northants Veggies
106 Eastfield Road, Wellingborough,
Northamptonshire NN8 1PA, tel
01933 381731, e-mail
jane.mills7@ntlworld.com

Wellingborough Veg Info Centre
Fieldview, 54 Grange Road, Redhill
Grange, Wellingborough,
Northamptonshire NN9 5YQ, tel
01933 674311

Nottingham Vegetarian & Vegan Society
245 Gladstone Street, Nottingham
NG7 6HX, tel 0845 458 9595, e-mail
nvvs@veggies.org.uk

Oxford Vegetarians
57 Sharland Close, Grove, Wantage,
Oxfordshire OX12 0AF, tel 01235
769425, e-mail oxfordveg@ivu.org

Oswestry Vegetarian Information Centre
Hobnob House, Maesbury Marsh,
Oswestry, Shropshire SY10 8JH, tel
01691 670404, webmaster@ivu.org

Shropshire Veggies & Vegans
1 Lees Farm Drive, Madeley, Telford,
Shropshire TF7 5SU, tel 01952 588878,
e-mail david.whalley@talk21.com

North Somerset Vegetarian & Vegan Info
Centre
6 Oakridge Close, Sidcot, Winscombe,
Somerset BS25 1LY, tel 01934 843853,
e-mail rogerhards@venusmead.go-
plus.net

4 Paws 1 Planet
Freshfields, School Bank, Hollington,
Stoke-on-Trent, Staffordshire ST10
4HH, tel 01889 507274, e-mail
hilary.dp@virgin.net

Lichfield District Vegetarian Info Centre
tel 07852 190855, e-mail
veggie@talktalk.net

Animals in Need (Woking)
7 Candlerush Close, Maybury,
Woking, Surrey GU22 8AT, tel 01483
871392, e-mail
david.rainford4@ntlworld.com

Croydon Vegetarians
  Flat 23, Zodiac Court, 165 London
  Road, Croydon, Surrey CR0 2RJ, tel
  020 8688 6325
Guildford Vegetarian Society (Surrey)
  Tel 01483 425040
Kingston & Richmond Vegetarians
  87 Porchester Road, Kingston-upon-
  Thames, Surrey KT1 3PW, tel 020
  8541 3437, e-mail
  walker@martinlake.plus.com
Twickenham & Surrey Vegetarian &
  Vegan Group
  tel 020 8941 8075, e-mail
  lesley@vegan4life.org.uk
Woking Veggie & Vegan Group (Surrey)
  wokingveg@aol.com
Arun and Worthing Vegetarian Info Centre
  (Sussex)
  tel 01903 775236, e-mail
  jvandepoll@aol.com
Lewes & Hastings Area Vegetarian &
  Vegan Group
  Sandhills Oast, Bodle Street, nr
  Hailsham, East Sussex BN27 4QU, tel
  01435 830150, e-mail jlj@mistral.co.uk
Reddy Veg
  39 Sallyport Crescent, Newcastle upon
  Tyne, Tyne & Wear NE1 2NE, tel
  0191 285 9980, e-mail
  MikeCasselden@blueyonder.co.uk
VegNE
  c/o Alternative Soles, 2 Alnwick
  Terrace, Wideopen, Newcastle upon
  Tyne, Tyne & Wear, tel 0191 236 4904,
  e-mail mark@alternativesoles.com
Coventry Vegetarians & Vegans
  (Warwickshire)
  257 Sovereign Road, Earlsdon,
  Coventry CV5 6LT, tel 024 7671 5040,

  e-mail cov.veggies@hotmail.com
Birmingham Vegetarians & Vegans
  54-57 Allison Street, Digbeth,
  Birmingham, West Midlands B5 5TH,
  tel 0121 353 2442, e-mail
  info@bvv.org.uk
Wolverhampton Veggies & Vegans
  102 Shaw Road, Blakenhall,
  Wolverhampton, West Midlands WV2
  0AH, tel 01902 451195
Wolves Veggies Info Centre
  73 Oak Street, Merridale,
  Wolverhampton, West Midlands WV3
  0AH, tel 01902 682550, e-mail
  wolvesveggies@yahoo.co.uk
Swindon Veggies & Animal Concern
  (Wiltshire)
  tel 01793 644796, e-mail
  denisvegan01@tiscali.co.uk
Redditch Vegetarians & Vegans
  PO Box 10202, Redditch,
  Worcestershire B98 8YT, tel 01527
  458395, e-mail reddiveggie@lycos.com
Bradford Veg Info Centre
  66 Kirkgate, Shipley, West Yorkshire
  BD18 3EL, tel 01274 598455, e-mail
  atmatrasi@btinternet.com
Leeds Vegetarian Society
  20 Berkeley Mount, Harehills, Leeds,
  West Yorkshire LS8 3RN, tel 0113 248
  4044, e-mail
  natleodis@googlemail.com
North Riding Vegetarians & Vegans
  Cottage no 3, Arrathorne, Bedale,
  North Yorkshire DL8 1NA, tel 0845
  458 4714, e-mail vegan@phonecoop.coop
Sheffield & District (South Yorkshire)
  tel 0114 230 4267, e-mail
  cheznous.post@virgin.net

South Yorkshire Vegetarian Group
e-mail mymitzi@lycos.co.uk

Scotland

Aberdeen Vegetarian Information Centre
17 Howburn Place, Aberdeen AB11
6XT, tel 01224 573034, e-mail
george_rodger1940@yahoo.co.uk
Clyde Coast (South) Information Centre
Old Sawmill Cottage, Kilkerran,
Maybole KA19 7PZ, tel 01655 740451,
e-mail kilkerran@breathemail.net
East Lothian Veggies
44 Gourlaybank, Haddington, East
Lothian EH41 3LP, tel 01620 823643,
e-mail elveggies@lindasneddon.co.uk
Edinburgh Vegetarians
45 Riverside Grove, Edinburgh EH12
5QS, tel 0131 623 0095, e-mail
jill@visualproducts.co.uk
Highland Veggies & Vegans
tel 01997 421109, e-mail
info@highlandveggies.org
Morayshire Vegetarian & Vegan Group
Hamewith, Mount Street, Dufftown,
Keith, Banffshire AB55 4FH, tel 01340
820292, e-mail ughamewith@aol.com
Scottish Borders Vegetarian Information
Centre
131 Roxburgh Street, Kelso TD5 7DU,
tel 0561 506751, e-mail
birderveg01@btconnect.com
South East Scotland Vegetarians
2 New Woodside, Bush Estate,
Penicuik, Midlothian EH26 0PH, tel
0131 445 1714, e-mail sesv@ivu.org
Tay Veggies
10 Hillpark Road, Wormit, Newport
on Tay, Fife DD6 8PR, tel 01382
541140, e-mail tayveggies@gmail.com

Wales

Bridgend Vegetarian Information Centre
2 Fairways, North Cornelly, Bridgend,
Glamorgan CF33 4DH, tel 01656
742008, e-mail bryn.mor@hotmail.co.uk
Caldicot Vegetarian Info Centre
1 Vicarage Gardens, Caerwent, nr
Caldicot, Gwent NP26 5BH, tel 01291
424984
Cardiff and the Vale Vegetarian Group
19 Pomeroy Street, Cardiff CF10 5GS,
tel 07790 742868, e-mail cardiff-vale-
vegetarians@hotmail.co.uk
Chester & Clwyd Vegetarian Group
Nant Yr Hafod Cottage, Hafod
Bilston, Llandegla, Clwyd LL11 3BG,
tel 01978 790442, e-mail
indesigneko@aol.com
Powys Vegetarian Info Centre
20 Ffordd Mynydd Griffiths,
Machynlleth, Powys SY20 8DD, tel
01654 702562, e-mail
dyfiguest@yahoo.co.uk
South West Wales Vegetarian Group
Glanrhydw Cottage, Cloigyn,
Pontantwn, Kidwelly, Carmarthenshire
SA17 5NB, tel 01267 232733, e-mail
grahamesme.goddard@btinternet.com

VisitBritain offices

Overseas readers: your nearest VisitBritain (previously the British Tourist Authority) office will be pleased to provide you with maps, guides and travel advice. General information as well as the offices' e-mail and website addresses can be found at www.visitbritain.com while the Britain and London Visitor Centre, 1 Regent Street, London SW1Y 4XT can help with travel information once you have arrived in this country.

AUSTRALIA
VisitBritain, Level 2, 15 Blue Street, North Sydney, NSW 2060

BELGIUM
Visit Britain, BP 25, 1040 Etterbeek 2

BRAZIL
VisitBritain, Centro Brasileiro Britanico, Rua Ferreira de Araujo 741, 1 andar, Pinheiros, Sao Paulo, SP 05428-002

CANADA
VisitBritain, 160 Bloor Street East, Suite 905, Toronto, Ontario M4W 1B9

CHINA
VisitBritain, c/o Cultural and Education Section British Embassy, 4/F Landmark Building Tower 1, 8 North Dongsanhuan Road, Chaoyang District, 100004 Beijing

VisitBritain, c/o British Consulate General Shanghai, 1st Floor Cross Tower, 318 Fu Zhou Lu, 200001 Shanghai

DENMARK
VisitBritain, Kristianiagade 8, 3., 2100 Copenhagen

FRANCE
VisitBritain, 5 étage, 7-13 Rue de Bucarest, Paris 75008. Post: Office de

Tourisme de Grande-Bretagne, BP 154-08, 75363 Paris Cedex 08

GERMANY
VisitBritain & Britain Visitor Centre, Dorotheenstrasse 54, 10117 Berlin

GREECE
VisitBritain, 29 Michalakopoulou Street, Athens 11528

HONG KONG
VisitBritain, 7/F The British Council, 3 Supreme Court Road, Admiralty

HUNGARY
VisitBritain, 1063 Budapest, Bajnok u. 19

INDIA
VisitBritain, 202-203 JMD Regent Square, 2nd Floor, Mehrauli Gurgaon Road, Gurgaon, Haryana – 122 001

VisitBritain, c/o British Council Division, British Deputy High Commission, Mittal Tower 'C' Wing, 2nd Floor, Nariman Point, Mumbai - 400 021

VisitBritain, c/o British Trade Office, Prestige Takt, 23 Kasturba Road Cross, Bangalore – 560 001

ITALY
VisitBritain, Via Cesare Cantù, 20123 Milano

JAPAN
  VisitBritain, Akasaka Twin Tower 1F,
  2-17-22 Akasaka, Minato-ku, Tokyo
  107-0052

MALAYSIA
  VisitBritain, c/o The British Council,
  Ground Floor, West Block, Wisma
  Selangor Dredging, 142C Jalan
  Ampang, 50450 Kuala Lumpur

NETHERLANDS
  Post: VisitBritain, Postbus 20650,
  1001 NR Amsterdam

NEW ZEALAND
  VisitBritain, c/o British Consulate-
  General Office, Level 17, IAG House,
  151 Queen Street, PO Box 105-652,
  Auckland

NORWAY
  Det Britiske Turistkontor, Dronning
  Mauds Gate 1, 0161 Oslo. Post: PB
  1554 Vika, 0117 Oslo

PORTUGAL
  VisitBritain Portugal, Largo Rafael
  Bordalo Pinheiro 16, 2o piso, sala
  210, 1200-396 Lisboa

RUSSIA
  VisitBritain, c/o The British Embassy,
  10 Smolenskaya naberezhnaya,
  121099 Moscow

SINGAPORE
  VisitBritain, 600 North Bridge Road,
  #09-10 Parkview Square, 188778

SOUTH AFRICA
  VisitBritain, Regus Bryanston, The
  Campus, Twickenham Building,
  Bryanston, 2021 Johannesburg. Post:

PO Box 67302 Bryanston 2021

SOUTH KOREA
  VisitBritain, c/o British Embassy,
  Taepyeongno 40, 4 Jeong-dong, Jung-
  gu, Seoul (100-120)

SPAIN
  Turismo Británico, PO Box 708, C/
  Columela 9 1 dcha, 28001 Madrid

SWEDEN
  Brittiska Turistbyrån, Klara Norra
  Kyrkogata 29, 111 22 Stockholm.
  Post: Box 3102, 103 62 Stockholm

THAILAND
  VisitBritain, c/o The British Council,
  254 Chulalongkorn Soi 64 Siam
  Square, Phyathai Road Pathumwan,
  Bangkok 10330

UNITED ARAB EMIRATES
  VisitBritain, 2nd Floor, Sharaf
  Building, Khalid Bin Waleed Road,
  Dubai. Post: PO Box 33342, Dubai

USA
  VisitBritain, 551 Fifth Avenue, Suite
  701, New York NY 10176-0799

  VisitBritain, 11766 Wilshire Blvd,
  Suite 1200, Los Angeles CA 90025